All These Things
into Position

Popology

SHORT THEOLOGICAL ENGAGEMENTS WITH POPULAR MUSIC

Series Editor: Christian Scharen

Editorial Committee: Margarita Simon Guillory, Jeff Keuss, Mary McDonough, Myles Werntz, Daniel White Hodge

Popology features theologians who have a passion for particular popular artists and who offer robust theological engagements with the work of that artist—engaging a song, an album, or a whole body of work over a career. Books in the series are accessible, yet deep both in their theological and musical engagement. Each book foregrounds ideas of interest in the musician's work, first, and puts these into conversation with the context and culture, second, and the Christian tradition, third. Each book, therefore, includes analysis of the cultural artifact, cultural context, and the relation to Christian tradition. Each book endeavors, as well, to speak with vitality to the challenges of living with God's mercy and justice in today's world.

All These Things into Position

What Theology Can Learn from
RADIOHEAD

Robert Cady Saler

with a foreword by Peter Bouteneff

 CASCADE *Books* · Eugene, Oregon

ALL THESE THINGS INTO POSITION
What Theology Can Learn from Radiohead

Popology: Short Theological Engagements with Popular Music

Cascade Books
An Imprint of Wipf and Stock Publishers
199 W. 8th Ave., Suite 3
Eugene, OR 97401

www.wipfandstock.com

PAPERBACK ISBN: 978-1-5326-0679-3
HARDCOVER ISBN: 978-1-5326-0681-6
EBOOK ISBN: 978-1-5326-0680-9

Cataloguing-in-Publication data:

Names: Saler, Robert Cady, author. | Bouteneff, Peter, foreword.
Title: All these things into position : what theology can learn from
    Radiohead / by Robert Cady Saler; foreword by Peter Bouteneff.
Description: Eugene, OR : Cascade Books, 2019 | Popology: Theologi-
    cal Engagements with Popular Music | Includes bibliographical
    references and index.
Identifiers: ISBN 978-1-5326-0679-3 (paperback) | ISBN 978-1-5326-
    0681-6 (hardcover) | ISBN 978-1-5326-0680-9 (ebook)
Subjects: LCSH: Radiohead (Musical group). | Religion and culture. |
    Popular music—Religious aspects.
Classification: LCC ML3921.8.P67 S2 2019 (print) | LCC
    ML3921.8.P67 (ebook)

Manufactured in the U.S.A.

Table of Contents

Series Foreword vii

Foreword by Peter Bouteneff *x*

Acknowledgments xvi

1. Introduction:
Aesthetics of Defiance 1

2. "We Are Just Happy to Serve":
Radiohead and the Church in the Marketplace 21

3. "The Best You Can Is Good Enough":
The Theological Refusal of Consolation 45

4. Radiohead and Salvation 70

5. "You Look So Tired":
Conclusion 90

Index 95

Table of Contents

Series Foreword

This first volume in the series Popology: Short Theological Engagements with Popular Music is such a lovely and compelling realization of what has been for so long just a dream. Our gratitude to Robert Cady Saler for bringing this vision down to earth, and in just the ways we envisioned now more than five years ago. The dream was to land a series somewhere between Oxford's well-known Very Short Introductions series whose volumes are smart, accessible, and original introductions to a wide range of subjects by well-known scholars, and the Bloomsbury 33 1/3 series, each volume written about a single album in the spirit of passionate music fandom. Add a layer of intentional theological depth and the specific mash-up we had in mind comes into view.

As the series description notes, we desire books that foreground ideas of interest to the musicians' work, first, seeking to take an account of their art on its own terms. Saler does this with a sophisticated and comprehensive sense of Radiohead's oeuvre, positioning their art as instructive for theology, with theology taking a distinctively humble role as learner, rather than the teacher. This is quite a reversal from the classic 20th century position articulated by, for instance, Paul Tillich who posited that culture asks questions to which theology formulates answers. Here, Radiohead's sophistication in its prophetic defiance, demur stance with regard to answers, and paradoxical embrace of both resignation and hope, come together to guide theology in a deeply human and honest engagement with the most pressing realities of our post-industrial, apocalyptic societies.

A second concern of the series, after in-depth attention to the musicians themselves, is to set the art in context, making the point that as in all art, popular music both reflects and offers commentary on its cultural milieu. Often, although certainly not always, art acts as a prophetic critique of culture, and in this case Radiohead delivers. While mostly oblique and without any formal religious or even prophetic self-understanding, Radiohead systematically takes on the planet-destroying industrial capitalist social order, a way of life that leaves the band and the listener with a "lingering malaise in the soul" as Saler puts it. We are, Radiohead argue in no uncertain terms, killing the planet, living unsustainably on the earth, and in need of both the courage of defiance and the imagination to see alternatives. For living these parallel modes, we have a superb soundtrack in this band.

The final concern for the series, after art and culture, is theology. In a fundamental sense, the series emerges from a recognition of the serious spiritual, moral, and even explicitly theological engagement in popular music. As the series unfolds, we will see artists who range from Radiohead, who are in no way explicitly theological, to other artists (say, Patti Smith, or The Roots) who do engage explicit theological themes in their work. Yet Saler deftly parlays Radiohead's clever and intentional engagement with themes of morality and, if you will, soul, as a means to say how theology and theologians have something to learn as they listen to the band. This perhaps is the hope for the series—to curate a vibrant conversation about the ways ordinary people and extraordinary artists alike are engaging the depths of life, seeking to make sense, and to find, as Radiohead does, a beating heart in the midst of God's beloved, broken, but ultimately beautiful, world.

Foreword

By Peter Bouteneff

Radiohead isn't an easy band to love. Its own members profess perplexity at their fans' affection for this odd music. Myself, I have listened to them a great deal over the past ten years, but until recently it felt a bit like eating kale: you know this stuff is really good for you, but the flavor and the mouth-feel make you wonder if it's worth it. Earlier this year, as I was descending the escalator at Madison Square Garden after another amazing Radiohead show, I thought to myself, "I admire this band endlessly. But do I *like* them?" Coming relatively late to this party—I wasn't raised on *OK Computer* and *Kid A*, and the alternative/grunge/electronica that were their initial context—I had some catching up to do. So even as I realized early on that they were brilliant and sui generis it took a good twenty listenings to that famous pair of albums until, quite suddenly, I began to enjoy them deeply, turning to them not out of a sense of artistic duty but for sheer pleasure. Radiohead isn't an easy sell—which is of course part of the allure for their audience, who adore them with a fervor that can be classified as, yes, religious.

One of their most admirable traits is their sense of detachment. They are capable of producing deeply likeable music, and perform it with zero shame or irony—the same spirit in which the fans eat it up. But perhaps their more default setting is one of musical sourness. They consistently draw us into an uncomfortable space, both lyrically and musically, and for some reason the fans eat that up at least as much as the "easy" material. Part of the explanation for that is their extraordinary musicianship: whether sweet or sour, refined or raw, the music is crafted with a composer's sensibility. Its pleasantness and its unpleasantness alike are delivered with originality, precision, and raw compositional talent. It is also honest, and absent of pretense. Detached.

This is how life ought to be. More specifically, it is how philosophy and religion should be, and still more specifically, it's how Christianity needs to be, and is at its best: beautiful and ugly, unflinchingly true both to the sweetness and the rot of our existence. Religion and its proponents have a lot to learn from that kind of honesty, and I say this in the spirit of this book's inspired subtitle. We theology/religion types are regularly (and rightly) ignored in the public square because our first question is too often "What can we teach the culture?" Whereas any message of worth, no matter who delivers it, is going to be all the more valuable if it is preceded by a deep listening. Of course, there can be a kind of utilitarian listening, where I am simply scanning for buzzwords and concepts within which to couch my message, to increase the likelihood of a surface resonance. But beyond any such cynical reasons for a listening posture, the fact is culture—the aggregated product of diverse human beings and communities—has something to teach. Unless your version of Christianity holds that people and their art are so far gone as to be totally depraved, then you trust that there's something positive to be learned virtually anywhere. That means it is worth listening closely, not just to "culture" writ large, but to culture that's as complex and unflinchingly truth-telling as Radiohead is. And so this book asks not what theology can teach Radiohead—who are doing fine, thank you—but what the phenomenon and music of Radiohead can teach theology and its practitioners.

As we "listen" in such a way to Radiohead, are we addressing more the words or the music? That question is always worth asking. Within rock, some bands care little or nothing about the words, and either murmur them (REM) or invent new languages that nobody's supposed to comprehend (Sigur Ròs). The music of other singer/poet/balladeers takes a distant back seat to the words (Dylan). With Radiohead it's both, and any book that is going to explore them for theological gleanings is going to spend a lot of time on lyrics. I've learned a lot from Saler's attentive listening and wise analysis. One of Radiohead's most ardent fans, and one of the most insightful theologians writing today, you can rightly expect him to sink deeply into the band's textual content, even as he's alert to the consonances and dissonances between lyrical message and its sonic vehicle. He also has a lot to say about the tensions between the band's cultural impact and their commercial success. His overarching insight—that Radiohead's music is often a tension between lyrics of devastating, pessimistic honesty and music pulsating toward hope—is profound. As for me, I tend toward ignoring a song's words unless they're right in my face: the only words I know from "Let Down" are "let down." So what I have to say pertains almost exclusively to the music itself, even as I know full well that the music wouldn't sound the way it does without the words and what they seek to express.

As you will be seeing as you dive into this excellent book, Christian theology has a lot to learn from Radiohead. To whet your appetite and begin generating ideas to build on, here are some of the "places" that I, as a theologian and a musician, look to learn from within this book.

One is their originality. No art comes out of nowhere, and Radiohead draws on a particular musical context, which also gives their listeners a toehold. But they are not beholden to a genre. That means that not only is their repertoire unlike anything else, but there are a large number of pieces that are not even remotely like anything else within their own oeuvre. While there is a kind of Radiohead home base we might associate with Thom Yorke's falsetto soaring over gritty guitars, orchestral electronics, and a solid groove, there is nothing like a single "Radiohead sound." Furthermore, there are compositions—like "Idioteque," "Myxomatosis," "Everything in its Right Place"—that are simultaneously unique within their repertoire and iconic within the whole of contemporary music.

I mentioned earlier their sense of detachment. That's probably related to what Rob Saler identifies as "defiance," but these come down to something more fundamental: *freedom*. When you are as talented as they are—and as locked in to each other, musically and ideologically—the scope of what you are able to say increases to near infinity. Yet the product of a talented, untethered, defiant artist isn't always going to be a good thing. And while there are audiences who enjoy being abused by the artists they admire, out of masochism or an illusion of what detached art looks like, art is better where there is . . . love. Without love, indie music is just a crashing cymbal. And in some mysterious and ever-increasing way, Radiohead's records and live shows convey something of love, of a totally un-sentimental variety.

The musical and lyrical effect of Radiohead is alienat-ing, but doesn't alienation presume the inner conviction that life can be, and at some level *is*, better than this? Add to this that sometimes the things that seem cold and dark are the very vehicles taking us into the light. A case in point is the role of technology in Radiohead's output. Their mu-sic frequently embodies the ways that technology takes us away from reality and engagement, and just as frequently switches around to bring technology to the service of mak-ing unbelievably beautiful sounds.

And this last point recalls what I said at the outset of this foreword, that one of the great gifts of Radiohead is their ability—and commitment—to be as true to the world's beauty and goodness as to its rot and sourness. Honesty, freedom, love, all those great things I've been touting above, won't have it any other way: you can't be *true* without doing justice to the glorious and the horrific. But you'll also show how the two can interrelate, bring-ing each other into sharper relief. You'll show, too, that the ugly can be a means of rising to beauty. And that's why ultimately it is beauty that prevails. Rob's book helps make that important point.

All of this is a standing lesson to "theology." It is a corrective of Christianities that are beholden to external norms, bereft of talent and creativity, resting on their own laurels, or forgetting love. It calls to mind the necessity of a non-conforming truth-telling that forbids theology from ignoring either joy or sadness, belonging or alienation, heaven or hell.

There's no band remotely like Radiohead. You couldn't possibly have thought them up. They are as insanely un-likely and dissonant as a faith whose loftiest redemptive moment is the voluntary death-by-torture of its messiah. And so, through this music that is just as often groovily compelling as it is acrid and alienating, comes one of the most potent affirmations of life and love you could ever hope for.

Acknowledgments

Radiohead fans are a contentious, weird, lovely, tight-knit, fractious, beauty-loving, and passionate community. So too are Christian theologians. To be a part of both communities for several decades has enriched my life tremendously, and so the first thanks go out to all of the fans of both the band and of the odd discipline known as academic theology. The genre of this text is best described as a nerdy fan letter to a band and to an in-house discussion among that surprisingly large Venn overlap between Radiohead fans and theology aficionados; if I've done at least some justice to both sides of the overlap, then I will be pleased.

A particular group of friends and colleagues exists at the intersection of love of music and love of theology, and I want to thank especially Zach Oster, Joel David Weir, Phil Goff, Elise Erikson Barrett, Frank Burch Brown, Adrian Bu, Jessica Mesman Griffiths, Jeffers Engelhardt, Jon Gill, Kyle Trowbridge, Burke Gertenschlager, Hanah Houser, Rob Distefano, and Peter Bouteneff (who wrote a lovely foreword) for many rich conversations about theology, aesthetics, and the places where pop culture meets the underground. Myles Werntz parlayed our collective online geekdom into an invitation to contribute this volume to this series, and I am grateful to him and to Chris Spinks (as well as the entire Cascade team) for editorial guidance.

This book was written almost exclusively beside a fireplace at the Blind Owl Brewery and Kitchen in Indianapolis, Indiana; long may its house flourish. Many thanks to the servers who knew when not to interrupt a good thought stream, and when to interrupt a bad one with another Belgian.

Portions of chapter 2 appeared originally as "Pastoral Care and Ecological Devastation: Un-Interpreting the Silence," *Journal of Lutheran Ethics* 16.2 (February 2016); and "The Earth, The Road, and the Tomb," *The Cresset* 77.3 (Lent 2013) 50–52; and are used with permission.

I've seen Radiohead live fourteen times (with a bonus five gigs with Atoms for Peace), but the most special was the time my sister brought me to Blossom Music Center in Cleveland, Ohio, and endured, in the front row center, an amazing set of music she didn't particularly care for just so I could be ecstatic the whole time. Thank you, Amanda Saler, and also Larry and Beth Saler, for your patient support of your son's esoteric research interests and similarly odd life choices. My children Cole and Nora, who are loved well and deeply by their mother Kristen, are the deepest influence upon my critical and existential decision to receive the music of Radiohead not as a soundtrack to despair but as a call to resist cynicism in the face of beauty; if not for myself, for them, and their world.

"Dedicated to all of you, and me . . . "

1

Introduction

Aesthetics of Defiance

I

On June 16, 2012, as Radiohead's crew was setting up the elaborate LED stage lighting system for the band's show in Downsview Park in Toronto, the stage suffered a collapse, injuring three and killing the tour's drum technician, Scott Johnson. The show was cancelled, the sellout crowd sent home, and the media speculated about whether the band would continue the globe-spanning tour behind their eighth album, *The King of Limbs*. Not only did the collapse damage their custom lighting system (a key component of their live show), but the trauma of losing their friend and crew member clearly struck deep among the band's members. On the band's website, drummer Phil Selway described the band as "shattered" by the loss. Lead singer Thom Yorke later stated that finishing the global tour was his toughest achievement as a band member.

The band first took the stage again several weeks after the accident, with a significantly pared-down set of screens and lights illuminating the stage. The setlists on the King of Limbs tour had, to that point, generally begun with the album's opener, "Bloom," which in live form—aided by the addition of a second tour drummer, Portishead's Clive Deamer—had become a polyrhythmic, propulsive launch to a high-energy set. As the band entered and took up their instruments, however, the visual and sonic landscape opening the set was very different.[1]

Under bare lighting, guitarist Ed O'Brien began scraping the top of his guitar neck above the bridge. Strumming in eighth notes filtered through a Boss reverb pedal, O'Brien slowly filled the arena with the ambient opener of "Lucky," a standout track from the album that took the band from relative alternative rock anonymity to critical acclaim, 1997's *OK Computer*. While on the King of Limbs tour the band regularly played the song as part of its sets, to open the show with it was unusual; indeed, it had not happened since 1998.

The lyrics quickly sent the contextual message: "Pull me out of the air crash . . . pull me out of the wreck." As the band conjured the horrors of machinery crushing flesh (a regular theme in Yorke's writing since the band's first album), the song's rousing affirmation—one of the few times in Radiohead concerts where the crowd is actively encouraged to sing along—"It's gonna be a glorious day," took on a whole new meaning. This was flesh, this was art, protesting against the impersonal forces—fate, machinery, modern technological existence—whose casualties sometimes come home in very personal ways. Mark Greif identifies such moments as notes of "defiance" as opposed to "revolution" in Radiohead's art:

1. As of the time of writing, the entire concert can be viewed via fan footage on YouTube: https://www.youtube.com/watch?v=NI_AE3fikvg.

> The difference between revolution and defiance
> is the difference between an overthrow of the ex-
> isting order and one person's shaken fist. When
> the former isn't possible, you still have to hold
> on to the latter, if only so as to remember you're
> human. Defiance is the insistence on individual
> power confronting overwhelming force that it
> cannot undo. You know you cannot strike the
> colossus. But you can defy it with words or signs.
> In the assertion that you can fight a superior
> power, the declaration that you will, this absurd
> overstatement gains dignity by exposing you,
> however uselessly, to risk. Unable to stop it in its
> tracks, you dare the crushing power to begin its
> devastation with you.

Greif goes on to argue that "at its best, Radiohead's music reactivates the moods in which you once noticed you ought to refuse. It can abet an impersonal defiance. This is not a doctrine the band advances, but an effect of the aesthetic."[2] As we will see throughout the book, this last point is crucial. For the most part, Yorke's lyrics are oblique and evocative enough to resist easy co-opting into a particular life philosophy or political agenda (with the possible exception of global climate change; more on that later). It is impossible to slot Radiohead as a "political act" in the same vein as their early contemporaries Rage Against the Machine, or as a quasi-spiritual act like their fellow arena-fillers U2. But, partly on the basis of this lack of one-to-one correspondence between art and agenda, the band is masterful at the art of defiance—the defiance

2. Mark Greif, "Radiohead, or the Philosophy of Pop," in *Radiohead and Philosophy: Fitter, Happier, More Deductive,* edited by Brandon W. Forbes and George A. Reisch (Chicago: Open Court, 2009) 30–31.

of the flesh against the machine, of the individual against the masses, perhaps even of life against death.

Anyone tempted to think that this was an overread of the opening of the show could have no doubts at the end. After its characteristic two-hour show, one that regularly earns the band high honors in the "Best Live Acts" category of music publications, the band added an uncharacteristic third encore. As images of Johnson were projected onto the screens above the band, Selway and Deamer launched into the bold opening percussion of "Reckoner"—a track from 2008's *In Rainbows*. Like many of Radiohead's songs— "Videotape," "Pyramid Song," "Paranoid Android"—the song features images of the afterlife and apocalyptic; unlike those tracks, however, "Reckoner" places the imagery in a sonically and lyrically hopeful key. Over a shimmering arpeggio and driving percussion, Yorke's falsetto soars: "Because we separate like ripples on a blank shore, in rainbows . . . take me with you."

The note sounded was not a religious one—no Radiohead members indicate a particular bent toward either organized religion or even "spirituality" in a recognizable sense. Unlike many ham-fisted religious "tributes" to departed souls, the implication was not that Johnson was now in some heaven that makes up for the tragedy of the loss. Such would be the sort of cheap religious consolation derided by Marx, Freud, Nietzsche, and others—religion as an opiate, a fantasy designed to make life on earth somehow more tolerable.

However, between "Lucky" and "Reckoner," and the hours of experimental rock bookended by these tracks, a different sort of affirmation could be discerned. Christian theologians often debate the necessary balance in theology between "transcendence" (the aspects of truth that

supersede what is evident to the senses and common experience) and "immanence" (the realities that are grounded
in material, concrete, "here and now" life as we experience
it). Increasingly, though, Christian thinkers have argued
that for Christians who worship a God made flesh in Jesus
Christ, the choice between truth in immanence and truth
in transcendence is ultimately a false dichotomy. Indeed,
it is IN and THROUGH deep immersion into the real
as such that ultimate truth—for Christians, God's own
truth—can be found.[3] We don't find truth by moving away
from the concrete earth into the ethereal heavens; we find
God by going as deeply into the real as God in Christ did.

To the extent that that is a sound theological principle, then the remarkable music and career of a resolutely
non-Christian band such as Radiohead becomes, as I will
try to show in this book, a helpful "soundtrack" for thinking Christian theology. The subtitle of the book, "What
Theology Can Learn from Radiohead," is important because we need to be clear from the outset that this book is
not a theology OF Radiohead, nor a book of theology that
seeks to mine Radiohead's music and lyrics for constructive theological ends. Unlike artists such as Bob Dylan,
Kanye West, etc., Radiohead is not a lyrics-driven band;
moreover, Radiohead provides few if any theologically rich
lyrics on par with those from Bruce Springsteen, Kendrick
Lamar, Lauren Hill, etc. What lyrics do come from Yorke's
pen rarely lend themselves to explicit God-talk; politics,
modern alienation, fragile relationships, and the brutality
of modern technology are the themes that come through
more often, and these in highly allusive and fragmentary
fashion. The most direct reference to God in Radiohead

3. For more on this theme in contemporary theology, see Robert
Saler, *Theologia Crucis: A Companion to the Theology of the Cross*,
Cascade Companions (Eugene, OR: Cascade, 2016).

lyrics comes in the lyrics to "Paranoid Android," in which (in the studio version) the muttered "God loves his children / God loves his children" replaced the demo's originals: "God loves his children / that's why he kills them." Trying to make Radiohead's art a source of theology in and of itself is a non-starter.

However, for the reasons listed above as well as ones that I hope to explore further in the book, Radiohead as a total phenomenon—musical, aesthetic, artistic, commercial—provides a great deal for theology to think WITH, or perhaps alongside. For Radiohead to "soundtrack" theology is for theology to consider how the extraordinary career of a band that has managed to retain critical acclaim while reaching global arena-filling status, a band that has found incredible success in the marketplace of contemporary popular music while resolutely following its own confounding muses, a band that leverages innovative technologies for both art and music-making while also sounding the alarm about the effects of technology upon the human spirit, can inform the work of theologians who must similarly seek to speak truthfully from particular social locations about God, humanity, and reality while navigating the demands of the structures of the marketplace of ideas (church, academy, publishing houses, etc.).[4]

Even more profoundly, as I will suggest, Radiohead's resolute refusal of cheap consolation, its aesthetically unswerving commitment to the depths of human suffering in a world coming apart under overlapping regimes of falsehood, bureaucracy, and indifference to catastrophe on an individual and global scale (such as climate change) sets an important standard for theology's own necessary

4. See Robert Saler, *Between Magisterium and Marketplace: A Constructive Account of Theology and the Church* (Minneapolis: Fortress, 2014).

commitments to authenticity in truth-telling.[5] Radiohead is a band that, on the whole, makes challenging, beautiful, and unrelentingly glum music—but the gulf between "glum" and "defiant" is one of many false opposites that the band's art undermines. If so much religion lends itself to excuses to close one's eyes to the world's need in favor of chimeric narratives of optimism ("the best you can is good enough"), then Radiohead's marshalling of beauty in the face of the crushing machine provides a soundtrack to hope—gritty, realistic, fragile hope.

As David Dark says, arguing for the "religious" character of Yorke's solo album *The Eraser*, "I would like to characterize the concerns of the album as ineluctably religious insofar as the songs bring, in an undeniable way, a profoundly ethical dimension to the quotidian dimensions the listener is already in, an emerging sense of responsibility animated by the demands of being (as well as receiving) a witness."[6] This is the province of theology that gives life rather than abets death. Contrary to its occasionally well-deserved reputation, theology should be an implacable opponent of bullshit. Radiohead is one source for teaching theologians what sustaining such opposition looks like. The point is less to provide answers and more to provide a soundtrack for theology to sustain itself as a decentered and de-centering discipline in the midst of the

5. For a powerful theological analysis of structural ecological damage as systemic sin, see Cynthia Moe-Lobeda, *Resisting Structural Evil: Love as Ecological-Economic Vocation* (Minneapolis: Fortress, 2013).

6. David Dark, "The Eraser: Start Making Sense," in *Radiohead and Philosophy: Fitter, Happier, More Deductive,* edited by Brandon W. Forbes and George A. Reisch (Chicago: Open Court, 2009) 88.

right questions—theology that is less about "everything in its right place" and more "like spinning plates." We need a witness.[7]

II

The stunningly beautiful 1995 track "Street Spirit," which closes both Radiohead's second album and (often) its concerts, provides another powerful example of this resistance in action. Over a sparse and delicate guitar line, aided eventually by strings, Yorke depicts once again the horrors of life physically crushed—"cracked eggs, dead birds, scream as they fight for life"—by impersonal forces: "this machine will not communicate." Amidst an almost palpable sonic sigh, Yorke repeatedly describes the alignment of these forces of impersonal machinery and death in language anticipating the influential opening of *Kid A*'s "Everything in its Right Place": "All these things into position, all these things into position." Brazilian theologian Vítor Westhelle has argued that, in the context of post-revolutionary Brazil, appeals to "order" in both political and theological discourse evoke images of military

7. Readers will notice throughout this text that, for the most part, "theology" for me is tied more or less directly to the ministry of the church. This is not to say that Radiohead has nothing to teach theologically that is not explicitly church-located; indeed, I imagine that theologians outside the institutional church can (and hopefully will) pick up on insights that are lost on those who, like myself, carry out our theological vocations firmly within church settings. But my particular interests, as I suspect will be apparent throughout the book, are around authenticity in proclaiming the gospel of hope over and against systemic forces of death, and in modes of community that form connection in an increasingly fragmented age, and I conceptualize both of those mainly in terms of the organized and visible Christian church.

dictatorship and fences keeping peasants from access to land,[8] and here Yorke's invocation of "into position" serves a similar purpose: throughout Radiohead's lyrics, imagery of order, tidiness, and proper positioning ("rows of houses") are ominous precisely because they are characteristic of the impersonal, Kafka-esque forces of bureaucracy that marshal death's "beady eyes" against vulnerable flesh. Against this backdrop, the repeated temptation comes to "fade out, fade out again." Let life be extinguished, or be numbed into oblivion with the narcotic distractions of modern life. "Fade out again."

But at the end of the song, buoyed by soaring orchestration and the gradual escalation of Yorke's vocals from sigh to near-yell, the singer closes with the plea: "Immerse your soul in love." On the surface, it is the most cliché sentiment of popular music: love is the answer, "all you need is love." Are we back to the threat of a cheap heaven, this time in the guise of vague "love," providing delusional consolation in the face of death?

Or, instead, does the very contrast between the relentless imagery of despair and the relative weakness and fragility of the affirmation of hope's possibility come to a head in the music itself? Kevin J. H. Dettmar argues that "the music of Radiohead doesn't just take alienation as a theme. . . . [R]ather, the songs of Radiohead stage this alienation, dramatically, as an almost epic battle between Thom Yorke's frail voice and the music which ultimately undergirds and overwhelms that voice."[9] Dettmar points

8. Vitor Westhelle, "Revelation 13: Between the Colonial and the Postcolonial, a Reading from Brazil," in *From Every People and Nation: The Book of Revelation in Intercultural Perspective,* edited by David Rhoads (Minneapolis: Augsburg Fortress, 2005) 183–99.

9. Kevin J. H. Dettmar, "Foreword," in *The Music and Art of Radiohead,* edited by Joseph Tate (Burlington, VT: Ashgate, 2005) xv.

out that this very dynamic provides the sonic key to another track from *The Bends*, "Fake Plastic Trees": "Having played out its sound and fury, the big-band sound gradually fades down, and 'Fake Plastic Trees' comes to a close on the stripped-down instrumentation with which it had opened; but Yorke's voice audibly quivers now, seemingly exhausted, spent, as he delivers the song's last lines. . . . Having replaced hubris with vulnerability. . . . Radiohead seems to have figured out a way to emerge victorious while singing of defeat."[10]

The attentive reader will notice a tension between these two strategies. Is the final affirmation in the face of crushing reality one of resistance, a sort of middle finger to the forces that crush life, or is it a kind of tragic and dignified resignation to the crushing that carries its own redemptive pathos and possibilities? Is the defiance in the fight or in the giving up, the refusal to play the game? This is, of course, the very tension that lies in the heart of Christian theology in its attempt to remain faithful to a crucified Messiah. Is the church called to be a militant and triumphant body, spreading its message and influence over the earth? Or is the call to Christian life one of following Christ to the cross in fidelity with crucified people across the world? Both? Neither? Radiohead's art does not provide an easy answer to this aporia, which is a clue that theology should not either. But lack of concrete answers does not mean lack of hope in the eventual triumph of life over death, either in the disciples' time or in ours.

For now, we can stipulate that the sonic juxtaposition of unrelenting lyrical honesty and musical pulsation toward something like hope will be a consistent theme throughout this book, especially when we move to the

10. Dettmar, "Foreword," xvi.

questions of theologically motivated activism and the christological shape of salvation in art.

Meanwhile, fans of Radiohead—and indeed, even the most casual observer of the landscape of post-1990's popular culture—will notice another emerging issue: in every possible sense, Radiohead itself is "in position" as one of the most dominant commercial forces in the music industry. Not only does the band routinely headline the world's biggest music festivals—Glastonbury, Lollapalooza, Coachella—and sell out arenas, its influence upon tastemaking bodies such as *Pitchfork* and its footprint in movies, television, and literature is significant. Put simply, the artists of Radiohead, by virtue of being part of one of the biggest bands in the world, are millionaires many times over on the basis of selling, not only music, but a vast array of merchandise via their own online store; meanwhile, any sense of their art as renegade or avant-garde needs to contend with the fact that few bands are more "mainstream" in terms of influence and exposure. Here, too, a parallel with Christianity suggests itself: the church ostensibly offers a gospel message that is often portrayed by its proponents as "countercultural," even as—since the fourth century onward—in large parts of the globe the church remains a dominant cultural and political force whose brokering of the message of the cross has often involved violence and repression. Is Radiohead the rebellion against the machines of late capitalism or part of the machine itself? Or both? And what, mutatis mutandis, of the church? And—as the book will take up time and time again—what do these dynamics mean for the ability of art and theology to foster hope amidst the machine?

III

This book seeks not so much to answer these questions as to take them as generative provocations toward explorations in theological content and method. Across the three essays that follow, three topics—the creation of authenticity in the midst of market forces, the interplay between hope and despair in truth telling, and the role of beauty in forming resistance to forces of death—will serve as windows into what it means for theology to think alongside Radiohead and learn from the band's work. The method will be dialogical—there are moments where Radiohead can teach theology, and moments where—from my theological vantage point—the Christian theological tradition(s) at their best can speak back constructively to augment and occasionally challenge the message of the art. Each essay can be read on its own; together they (hopefully) form a window into how Radiohead continues to find what I would call the *beating human heart within the machine*, and how Christian theology might do the same. A recurring theme throughout the book will be the fate of truth, beauty, and meaning under the economic conditions of neoliberalism, the intentional yet organizationally diffuse commodification of everything under the belief that market forces shape reality benevolently.[11] Another theme will be how Radiohead's juxtaposition of unrelenting lament at the brokenness of our planet and the societies on it with intense musical beauty provides a kind of template for how Christian theology can engage unvarnished reality with something like authentic hope. And, finally, at work in the pages is the search for authentic community, traditional or

11. See Adam Kotsko, *Neoliberalism's Demons* (Stanford: Stanford University Press, 2018).

otherwise, that allows for the aesthetics of defiance to be lived communally and not alone.

Of course, to even speak about the "message" or import of a given aspect of the Radiohead phenomenon is to imply critical interpretation on my part, and thus the book also serves as an intervention into ongoing debates within musicological and cultural criticism as to the meaning of the band's art. My own disciplinary vantage point is that of specifically Christian theology and not musicology per se; thus, while the book will draw on relevant insights from various disciplines, the intended contribution is theological through and through. While I hope the discussions will be of interest to Radiohead fans more broadly, large sectors of the book will be devoted to theology inspired by/ in conversation with the band's art rather than in-depth analysis of the art itself. I also pretend no objectivity as regards my subject matter on either front. I am an unabashed longtime Radiohead fan, and I am a (bad) Christian who believes that theological claims about truth, meaning, and hope in the world's redemption point to realities that both transcend and suffuse our broken world. I would like to think what follows in these pages will be of some interest to those who share all, some, or perhaps even none of my convictions about the quality of Radiohead's music or the veracity of Christian claims, but I leave that to others to determine.

Note: Radiohead is one of the very few acts in modern rock that has maintained the exact same membership lineup for its entire two decade plus career. While occasionally employing auxiliary musicians (such as Deamer) for touring, the lineup of Thom Yorke, Ed O'Brien, Jonny Greenwood, Colin Greenwood, and Phil Selway has been consistent from their first EPs to the present, with no significant breaks in writing, touring, and recording throughout their entire history. Thus, while in this book I might occasionally single out a given member's contributions (e.g. Yorke's lyrics, Greenwood's guitar, etc.), for the most part I will refer to "Radiohead" as a singular unit. Their extraordinary collaboration and longevity merits this authorial positioning when it comes to their art.

As regards the band itself, there are many excellent biographies of the men from Oxford available in both print and online form.[12] In keeping with my desire to have this book focus with intensity on the question of what theology can learn from the total phenomenon of the band—its art, its marketing, its aesthetic—apart from a brief sketch below I will not rehash much in the way of biography, discography, etc. The book is about theology in conversation with Radiohead, with any contribution to broader Radiohead scholarship standing as a happy accident but an accident nonetheless.

To my delight in researching the topic, Radiohead has received significant scholarly attention, with monographs from major university presses (Oxford, Indiana University, etc.) as well as influential alternative presses (not to mention a plethora of online and print discussions in fan forums, music magazines, etc.). Doctoral dissertations, major conference presentations, and interdisciplinary studies of the band continue to pick up steam. To my knowledge, little of this critical attention has been explicitly theological in nature, and so in some respects this book proceeds on experimental ground. But in a larger sense the book joins a broad, multi-disciplinary conversation about this important band, and that is both a challenge

12. See especially Mac Randall, *Exit Music: The Radiohead Story*, updated edition (Milwaukee: Hal Leonard, 2012).

and a thrill. For the purposes of readability in what follows I will do my best to keep excessive citation to a minimum; however, I trust that my indebtedness to others who have written on Radiohead and God and everything in between will be clear throughout.

IV

Before diving into the book, we might get some sense of the arc of Radiohead's career and oeuvre.

The band began in 1985 at Abingdon School in Abingdon, Oxfordshire. The original members—Thom Yorke, Jonny Greenwood, Colin Greenwood, Phil Selway, and Ed O'Brien—initially called themselves "On a Friday" (named after their practice time). They were supported and mentored by music teacher Terence Gilmore-James. After playing their first gig at Oxford's Jericho Tavern, they eventually rode enthusiasm for Britpop alternative to a deal with EMI Records Ltd. It was on EMI's advice that the band changed their name to Radiohead, a title taken from a relatively obscure track by the band Talking Heads.

Radiohead's first commercial enterprise, their debut EP *Drill*, did not achieve widespread success initially; nor did their first hit "Creep," which debuted as a single in 1992 and was released as part of their first album *Pablo Honey* in 1993. British audiences were largely negative about the song and the band, but international markets—particularly those of Israel, where the band played their first international show, and of the United States, where "Creep" became a national hit—responded to the song in a way that opened up touring opportunities abroad and slowly created respect at home.

Soon after the release of *Pablo Honey*, the band released a second EP—*My Iron Lung* in 1994—and a second album, *The Bends* in 1995. *The Bends* is widely hailed as a massive improvement over the debut, and a number of tracks from the album—"Fake Plastic Trees," "Just," and "Street Spirit"—remain staples of the band's live show. This period saw the band touring with one of their most significant musical inspirations, REM, and also finding increasing success in the music video realm. To a greater extent than their fellow countrymen Blur and Oasis, Radiohead found a comfortable niche within the emerging grunge/alternative movements in the US and elsewhere. This album also was the first in which the band worked with producer Nigel Godrich, who subsequently became so synonymous with the band's sound that he is often considered a de facto member.

In 1997, *OK Computer*—the album considered by many to be Radiohead's masterpiece—was released. *OK Computer*, based loosely on a science fiction narrative about an alien coming to earth and encountering the vacuity of modern life, was both critically and popularly acclaimed. The last of the unambiguously guitar-heavy Radiohead records thus far, the album melded sonic experimentation with angsty alt-rock aggression shot through with moments of quiet beauty. Radiohead accompanied their release of *OK Computer* with a grueling worldwide tour, about which a documentary—*Meeting People Is Easy*—was made. The band soon graduated from playing mid-size clubs to headlining festivals and even arenas. Meanwhile, the *OK Computer* album itself is archived in the Library of Congress for its historical significance.

The hectic schedule necessitated by their album's success and the rigors of touring—in particular, press relations—caused stress and strain within the band. As they realized they were in danger of breaking up, Radiohead decided to take a break from performing rather than push themselves to the breaking point. They stopped producing music until 1999, when the band began to work on recording what would be *Kid A* and *Amnesiac*—two distinct albums recorded in the same sessions.

Though the albums were worked on simultaneously, *Kid A* was released in 2000 and *Amnesiac* was released in 2001. These albums marked a change in Radiohead's sound, becoming even more experimental and incorporating electronic influences in a way that was more pronounced than in their earlier albums. This change garnered mixed reviews from fans, many of whom were not expecting this stylistic shift. Having purchased the entire Warp Records catalogue, Thom had clearly become more intrigued by experimental electronic and dance music than guitar rock proper, and the band appeared to be following along. Hailed as one of the first mainstream "post-rock" albums, *Kid A* marked a significant departure that would influence hundreds of bands similarly intrigued by the possibilities of transmogrified song structures in mainstream music. *Amnesiac*, meanwhile, while derided by some as an insignificant collection of b-sides, soon became a litmus test for true Radiohead fandom—among fans, acknowledgment that "Pyramid Song" and "Like Spinning Plates" are vastly superior to radio hits such as "Creep" and "High and Dry" is, for better or for worse, *de rigeur*.

The band's one officially released live album, *I Might Be Wrong*, was released in 2001. From a band known for playing two and a half hour shows with multiple encores, the eight-track EP was a bit of an oddity—short, encompassing only material from *Kid A* and *Amnesiac* (a subtle jab, perhaps, at rock-oriented critics who speculated that the electronically influenced material would never translate into a live setting?). The album does contain two undeniable highlights: the piano-driven live interpretation of "Like Spinning Plates" and a previously unreleased acoustic track, "True Love Waits." Extensive trade in Radiohead bootlegs, meanwhile, remains an Internet hobby of many a fan.

Radiohead's next full album, *Hail to the Thief*, was released in 2003 after international tours in Spain and Portugal in which the band played many of the songs which would appear on the album. *Hail to the Thief* maintained the band's newfound complexity while crafting a sound more recognizable to fans of their earlier works, as well as bearing a number of intense political jabs at the emerging hawkish climate in the US and UK (the title is likely a reference to the perception of George W. Bush "stealing" the popular vote in the US presidential election the year prior). While the album is a favorite among certain Radiohead fans and contains some of their most compelling tracks—"There There" and "Myxamatosis" remain live favorites—the album also contained enough weak tracks to leave the band wishing that they had spent more time on sequencing and editing the album, perhaps even releasing it as a shorter EP. The *Hail to the Thief* tour encompassed headlining slots on some of the world's largest music festivals as well as large-scale shows held in tents devoid of corporate logos.

From 2003 to 2006, Radiohead refrained from performing—Jonny focused on classical composition, Thom continued to cultivate his love of electronic music, and the other band members largely attended to family matters. The band returned in 2007 with *In Rainbows*, their first album released after the end of their contract with EMI Records (eventually the album was released on XL Recordings). *In Rainbows* was released digitally as a pay-what-you-want album in October of 2007 and released as a physical record months later—in December on international release and January of 2008 in the United States. The "pay what you want" schema (in which, upon ordering the album, fans were given a box saying "it's up to you" when they went to pay) made international news and began an ongoing trend of artists giving their music away free on the Internet in exchange for tour buzz, sales of physical albums, etc. As far as the music itself, the album was widely regarded as the best and most accessible Radiohead album since the *OK Computer/Kid A* duo. The album was a massive success at a time when many assumed that the band's prime would have been over. The acclaim may have been due in part to the band emphasizing a return to guitar and piano-based rock at a level that could draw in new fans while offering enough complexity to satisfy veteran listeners. The band also stepped up its climate change advocacy at this time, with Thom in particular vocally supporting a number of environmental causes (more on this in chapter 2 below).

Just over three years after the release of *In Rainbows*, Radiohead released *The King of Limbs* both digitally and physically with very little advanced notice—a move that had become a signature for the band since the *In Rainbows* release as well as the low-key release of Thom's first solo album, *The Eraser*. Radiohead announced the album on Valentine's Day 2011, only four days before the February 18 release. This album also marked the inclusion on tour of second drummer Clive Deamer, who has since joined the band on their other tours. The album itself was largely considered underwhelming—the popular music site *Pitchfork*, long understood to be an unwavering advocate of the band, gave it a lukewarm review, and fans were disappointed by its short length and largely derivative tracks ("Lotus Flower," in particular, seemed a paler version of "There There"). Live, however, the addition of Deamer and Thom's ongoing interest in Afrobeat music inspired the band to amplify the tracks with polyrhythmic complexity, nastier guitar tones, and more overall percussive force, and the results were positive. *King of Limbs'* tracks remain good live fodder even if their recorded versions seem flat by comparison.

Between 2012 and 2014, members of Radiohead largely worked on solo projects (Thom's side project with Flea entitled Atoms for Peace, Jonny's composition work, Phil Selway's solo albums, etc.). They began to work on *A Moon Shaped Pool* in 2014. An overall "quiet" album that synthesized a number of tracks played on the *King of Limbs* tour, Thom's solo tracks, and a studio version of the aforementioned fan favorite "True Love Waits," the album was a much more significant commercial and critical success than *King of Limbs*, even though some fans continue to wish for more straightforward rock tracks such as those revisited on *In Rainbows*. The album also featured Deamer in the studio, thus making him a new regular member of the band. As of this writing, the *Moon Shaped Pool* tour is continuing throughout the summer of 2018.

2

"We Are Just Happy to Serve"

Radiohead and the Church in the Marketplace

I

Is there a market for truth? Is there a market for beauty? The question can, of course, cut both ways. One way of reading it would be to ask Can genuine truth and beauty sell? The reverse, though, also prompts us to question, To what extent does the determination of what is true and beautiful depend on what will sell? Is the problem about whether there is a market for real art, or whether the market is the ultimate ground of what is real in art?

People by the millions pay millions to buy Radiohead. Buy their music (even universally acknowledged weaker albums such as *The King of Limbs* go platinum multiple times over), buy their concert tickets at levels allowing them to headline the largest arenas and music festivals (such as Glastonbury and Lollapalooza), buy branded merchandise ranging from the usual shirts and caps to baby onesies, water bottles, and custom afghans—all from their specially curated online shop, W.A.S.T.E. Their much-vaunted gestures at marketplace subversion—such as their instituting a "pay what you want" scheme for their *In Rainbows* album—end up becoming case studies, not only for music publications such as *Pitchfork* and *Rolling Stone*, but also business journals such as *Forbes* and *Billboard*.[1]

All this leads to the mildly suspicious line of questions posed well by Davis Schneiderman, who notes the instability of "sentiments suffused into the cataract of instrumentality that surrounds all of Radiohead's attempts to destabilize corporate culture." As he asks,

> Yorke may "sing" about the plight of the economic subject in "Dollars and Cents" ("We are the dollars and cents / and the pounds and pence / and the mark and the yen, and yeah / we're going to crack your little souls"), but how can we be sure that Radiohead, for all its deliberately muddled articulation and innovative studio work, is not a tool of this same endlessly looping beat of the marketplace?[2]

Schneiderman's uneasy inquiry is particularly incisive in that it lands precisely at the musicological fulcrum between "experimental" and "popular" art: the more Radiohead engages in sonically difficult experiments such as muddled vocals and atonal studio effects, the more their mythos grows and becomes sellable precisely as "cool." The tribe who "gets" it (and who then gets it with money) is

1. As Douglas Wolk writes, "The punch line is that, despite Radiohead's all-permeating abhorrence of the ultimate rock-band banality, the consumerist machine . . . they've got a more finely honed brand identity than any other band of the moment." Quoted in Marvin Lin, *Kid A*, 33 1/3 (New York: Bloomsburg, 2011) 90.

2. Davis Schneiderman, "'We Got Heads on Sticks / You Got Ventriloquists': Radiohead and the Improbability of Resistance," in *The Music and Art of Radiohead*, edited by Joseph Tate (Aldershot, UK: Ashgaste, 2005) 17.

sonically formed for consumption. As Marianne Letts puts it, rather polemically:

> Radiohead's highly successful marketing strat-
> egy appears to be centered around creating
> riddles for fans to try to solve. . . . By being de-
> liberately obscure in its presentation, Radiohead
> creates a community of followers who gain in-
> sider status by sharing and debating the clues left
> behind by the band. In addition, by creating an
> air of mystery in the presentation of its product,
> as well as decrying the very system upon which
> its ultimate financial success depends, the band
> cleverly builds demand by aligning itself with
> its audience against the record industry and
> elevates its art above mere "pop music" into the
> realm of the intelligentsia; only the astute can
> interpret the music's true meaning, and attempt-
> ing to do so initiates the listener into an insider
> network of people outside the mainstream.[3]

What does this mean?

II

This may seem like a premature line of questioning in the course of this book. A more standard order for a book like this would involve analyzing and appreciating Radiohead's art in order to suss out themes of truth, beauty, meaning, etc., and *then* to ask how these supposedly transcendental themes "survive" being commodified within the arena of the marketplace. This would imply that the music exists in a pure state prior to, and transcendent of, its status as

3. Marianne Letts, *Radiohead and the Resistant Concept Album: How to Disappear Completely* (Bloomington: Indiana University Press, 2010) 43–44.

performance and commodity. But putting issues of com-modification, marketplace dynamics, and the role of sup-posed "resistance" art that is sold and bought on a massive global scale front and center makes the very point that most needs making: there IS no separating Radiohead's art from its performance as commerce.[4] To pretend that the art possesses an aura of pre-commercial authenticity that only enters the marketplace in a utilitarian (or worse, tragically necessary) fashion rather than as constitutive of the performance itself is to commit two errors. The first is to exempt the band and its art from the vagaries of global commodification and "performance" of authenticity that bedevil the Radiohead phenomenon in a manner perhaps uniquely intense among contemporary popular musicians. In other words, it's to be naïve about just how inseparable Radiohead is from its status as rock commodity. The sec-ond error (and a flip side of the first) is to miss the effect of the band's seemingly self-aware navigation of this very dynamic, and their ability to turn this canny navigation into a constructive feature (not a bug) of its art. Moreover, both of these errors have an impact upon how Radiohead

4. Letts again:
   If a person or group's creative goal is presumed to be an artistic statement that exists above and/or superfluous to the corporate culture that will ultimately receive and promote it, then packaging that statement to sell back to the consumer, in the process making money off the very people with whom the artist claims to identify . . . is the ultimate irony. Yorke has underscored his consciousness of the band's place within the capitalist system with his decla-ration that "you're lying if you're pretending it's not a prod-uct, that you're not trying to sell something." Obviously conscious of the hurdles involved in negotiating corporate culture, in this statement Yorke reveals the man behind the curtain, creating the smoke and mirrors of anticapitalism while still reaping benefits from the products' sales. (Letts, *Radiohead and the Resistant Concept Album,* 43).

can teach theology about the agon and agonies of the marketplace as a venue for beauty and truth. They limit the potential for Radiohead to "soundtrack" theology well.

Let's explore each of these errors in turn.

Regarding the error of exemption: no one can claim that the ambiguities of music sold as commodity are unique to Radiohead. Any musician, from the singer-songwriter gigging at a local coffee shop to Beyoncé headlining Coachella has to reckon with the realities of marketing, economics, mass vs. niche appeal, etc. when it comes to the business of music. But Radiohead, by its own way of carrying itself and its art within a rapidly shifting marketplace—from the compact discs and A&R reps of the early '90s milieu in which the band started to the advent of indie rock's popular explosion, streaming music services, and indeed the Internet as a whole—forces the conversation in particularly intense ways. Their 1998 documentary, *Meeting People is Easy*, is largely an extended visual meditation on the complexities of emerging rock stardom and the exhausting grind of touring and media presentation; ironically (or not), the film only enhanced the band's status as critical and commercial darlings. As mentioned above, long before it became commonplace for artists to give their music away on the web (or, in the case of one prominent band, force their substandard new album onto unsuspecting iPhone owners everywhere), the early-morning announcement that the *In Rainbows* album would be made available by means of a "pay what you want" download fee (as well as an $80 deluxe box set, for those so inclined) grabbed both music critic *and* music industry headlines for weeks.[5] The band's 2003 tour

5. The question of whether Radiohead's eventual move from a major label to an independent one mitigates these concerns is usefully taken up by D. E. Wittkower, "Everybody Hates Rainbows," in

behind the *Hail to the Thief* album, in a visual scheme influenced by Naomi Klein's book *No Logo*, featured shows held in advertisement-free tents designed to immerse the thousands of fans who had paid the Ticketmaster fees and airfare to attend in a seemingly anti-corporate bubble.

We might put the question this way, using the analogy of inoculation, Do Radiohead's gestures toward subversion of corporate popular music culture serve as a sort of superficial catharsis that inoculates their fans—and perhaps themselves—from more searching interrogation? Does the protest actually help convince the fans that "get it" that they are somehow superior to fans of, say, Taylor Swift, even though from an industry standpoint (even if not a musical standpoint) Radiohead and Swift are largely different stores within the same mall?

But problematics are not always problems; complex issues are not always weaknesses. In fact, the reverse is often the case, and hence the second reason to put these difficult questions around art and commerce front and center in this book—*especially* in a book devoted to how an enterprise (namely, Christian theology and church life) that generates trillions of dollars annually across the globe can learn from Radiohead.[6] Our planet is inheriting a two-thousand-year-plus legacy—much of it brutal—of European-centered Christendom, and as various forms of Christian life explode in the global South many

---

Radiohead and Philosophy: Fitter, Happier, More Deductive, edited by Brandon W. Forbes and George A. Reisch (Chicago: Open Court, 2009) 123–34.

6. See Kathryn Lofton, *Consuming Religion* (Chicago: University of Chicago Press, 2017) for a pop culture–savvy argument that religion itself in the modern West can be understood as a way of orienting patterns and communities of consumption within the neoliberal global marketplace.

sociologists predict a "next Christendom" that has at its center raw numbers and global influence stemming from Latin America, Africa, and Asia. Christianity—its doctrines, its theologies, its institutions, its artistic production, its popular influence—operates on a global economic scale that dwarfs even large multi-national companies.

And just as Radiohead's art operates a space within the marketplace "selling" a vision of uncompromising artistic integrity, Christianity as a missionary religion has transformed entire cultures on the basis of a proclamation concerning an ignobly crucified Galilean peasant rabbi given Messianic status by his followers and sent to liberate, not just his people, but the entire world from deeply entranced forces of slavery and death. Paul, whose shaping of Christianity predates even the gospel narratives, rhetorically trades on the weakness and implausibility of the core Christian message in shoring up his own authority to speak in contested territory. In a letter to the Corinthians, Paul appeals to the fact that, in contrast to those who came to the churches with impressive appearance and speech, he is more akin to the crucified Jesus in that he presents weakness in order to let God's strength shine through: "For I decided to know nothing among you except Jesus Christ, and him crucified. And I came to you in weakness and in fear and in much trembling. My speech and my proclamation were not with plausible words of wisdom, but with a demonstration of the Spirit and of power, so that your faith might rest not on human wisdom but on the power of God" (1 Cor 2:2–5). Later, he points out that most of the members of these churches are similarly unimpressive people; like Paul, their weakness mirrors the weakness of the broken Christ on the cross precisely so that they might reflect the peculiar wisdom of God rather than human standards, since "God chose what is foolish in the world

27

to shame the wise; God chose what is weak in the world to shame the strong; God chose what is low and despised in the world, things that are not, to reduce to nothing things that are, so that no one might boast in the presence of God" (1 Cor 1:27–28). Paul, the apostle of the crucified, sees the essence of the church as that of a community whose weak members bear a weak message that nonetheless reveals the odd strength of God and God's methods for saving the world.

So we might say, borrowing Letts's remarks above, that Christianity too trades on a form of community-forming outsiderhood, an esotericism within the mainstream that adopts an obscure and interpretation-begging aesthetic in order to form strong lines between those who get it and those who do not. There is a crucial difference, however, and intriguingly Letts borrows theological language to articulate part of it. She argues that Radiohead's deployment of this community-forming obscurity is a "Gnostic" aesthetic.[7] Gnosticism, in the first few centuries CE, is a catch-all term for a variety of beliefs that regard the body as a prison of the soul that can only be released by means of secret knowledge ("gnosis") that is vouchsafed to an elect few. What became Christian orthodoxy opposed Gnosticism precisely because it was elitist; in the minds of Paul and others, truth should be available to all regardless of status, education level, virtue, etc. The truth may be sublime and require interpretation, but the community formed should strike a balance between being initiated into the mysteries (as in the catechumenate preparing candidates for baptism and the Eucharist) and yet in principle open to all.

7. Letts, *Radiohead and the Resistant Concept Album*, 44.

What does such community look like in today's marketplace of religions and meaning? And what can the phenomenon of community around rock music and Radiohead's art show us about how the church can live out this tension in generative ways?

III

> This is the essential paradox of the indie/alternative mentality: it thrives on difference, alienation, and otherness; and yet all these alienated others enjoy meeting up in fields to proclaim their otherness, etc., to a whole bunch of people who are dressed pretty much the same. Can a song still function as a soundtrack to loneliness if everyone appears to know all the words?[8]

We might take this question from Tim Footman as a sort of leitmotif as I take the liberty of sharing a snapshot of impromptu community from the life of a typical Radiohead fan—namely, myself.

The year is 2008, and it is 3 a.m.. My eyes have shot open unbidden, and I walk over to my computer screen. I do not yet have a smartphone, so in order to fuel this particular addiction I at least have to leave my bed and walk twenty steps or so (first world problems). I am making this pilgrimage with determination born of a distinct combination of desire and spite. A few years earlier, Radiohead had played a series of small theater gigs as a stopgap tour between *Hail to the Thief* and *In Rainbows*, and they had hit an intimate, acoustically amazing theater in my

8. Tim Footman, *Radiohead—Welcome to the Machine: OK Computer and the Death of the Classic Album* (Surrey: Chrome Dreams, 2007) 74.

city of Chicago. At the time the tickets for the Chicago gig went on sale, I was a casual fan of the band (*Kid A* had soundtracked a number of late night writing sessions in college, but that was about it). I was, however, a devoted fan of the Chicago live music scene, and I was also proud of my track record of jumping on hot tickets the second they went on sale. So, the morning of the 10 a.m. onsale, I logged in at 9:59 a.m., pulled up my Ticketmaster account, flexed my fingers, and hit the "Add Tickets" button the instant the screen for them came up.

Nothing. Sold out.

Granted, it was a smaller theater in a major metropolitan area. Granted, as I would later discover as I learned more about the economics of the concert industry, the combination of fan club presales, VIP, corporate seats, and so on meant that only a fraction of the venue's seats remained to be had at the time of the "general public onsale." Granted all that—still, the tickets had been scooped up in a fraction of a second. As a grad student, I had barely had the funds for face value tickets—no way could I pay hundreds to touts on the secondary market. I would be missing what at that time I mainly just knew as the hot band in town.

Embarrassingly, it was that proto-FOMO (Fear of Missing Out) that would give me the push I needed in 2007 to take a deep dive into Radiohead's catalogue—while I had respected the band from a distance before, I had not yet had occasion to fall in love. So I set about falling in love.

It worked. I fell in love with the music. But, as numerous cultural commentators have suggested, music consumption (particularly in this Internet age) is identity formation. Enjoyment of Radiohead's music soon parlayed itself into my becoming a Radiohead Fan—documentaries, bootlegs, shirts, chat rooms, setlist trainspotting, webcasts, the works. And with the territory of FanBoyDom came the straight-faced assertion that Radiohead was "the best live band in the world"—an assertion I made with a confidence fully unshaken by the fact that I had never, in fact, seen the band live.

Let's be clear: Radiohead fandom is intense. We don't have to stipulate that it is uniquely intense; the rock band Tool, for instance, is another massive band with a following devoted to esoterica about the band and its cryptic communications. But Radiohead fans are legendary for their fierce devotion to the band. The rock site *Pitchfork*, for instance, featured an infamous review of *Kid A* which actually contains the following sentence: "The experience and emotions tied to listening to *Kid A* are like witnessing the stillborn birth of a child while simultaneously having the opportunity to see her play in the afterlife on IMAX."[9] Radiohead fans are not playing around when it comes to expressing devotion.

Cue the magical morning of October 1, 2007, when a simple online message from Jonny Greenwood announced that the new album *In Rainbows* would be released via the then-unprecedented "pay what you want" model just nine days later. As a grad student dealing largely in ancient texts, I was at the time so non-tech savvy that the FLAC download system for the album intimidated me—I actually went on eBay to buy a burned CD of the album's tracks to play on my soon-to-be-extinct CD player. I sat and listened to the blissfully disorienting opening percussive stabs of "15 Step," the deceptively grunge-y riffs of "Bodysnatchers," the push-pull of menace and beauty in "All I Need," and

9. Brent Discrescenzo, "Kid A," *Pitchfork*, October 2, 2000, https://pitchfork.com/reviews/albums/6656-kid-a/.

I soon had two questions formed: which superficial critics will mistake this for a Coldplay-influenced album (a stupidly high number, as it sadly turned out)? And, when would the tour be?

The latter question was very much front and center at AtEase, the rabid online fan forum (the title comes from a lyric in "Fitter Happier") which had become my go-to online stop for debating lyrics, arguing for the salvageability of certain tracks off the band's much-maligned *Pablo Honey* debut (n.b. that "Blow Out" is as good as anything from *The King of Limbs* and then some), and to speculate about tour announcements. The hiatus between the *Hail to the Thief* tour and the new album had meant that, while a number of AtEasers were Radiohead concert veterans, many were in my shoes—loving a band with an incredible live reputation without ever having seen a show.

I have to stress again, for those who at this point might understandably be rolling their eyes, for a certain kind of fan, music consumption simply is identity formation. So much more was at stake than a few hours of live rock enjoyment; what was at stake was fandom as an orienting identity, a sense of having a handle upon the self-curation that is our opportunity and our curse in an age of "everything all of the time" ("Idioteque"). It is without question a dumb, privileged, neoliberal need, but it is none the less real—and in our time, perhaps all the more real—because of that.

It must have been on an AtEase thread that the announcement first came—the *In Rainbows* tour would hit dozens of worldwide cities, including multiple dates in the US. Even though the venues would be much larger this time, the horror stories of being shut out by the entity increasingly known as "TicketBastard" were fresh. So the obvious answer was the ever-elusive fan presale tickets from W.A.S.T.E.

If W.A.S.T.E., as noted above, is an imposing edifice of evil-teddy-bear themed band merchandise anyway, then its ticketing system is particularly wild. At the time of the *In Rainbows* tour, the rumors were flying that the tickets could go on sale at any moment without warning, with those of us in the US having the added excitement of a six-hour time change. The message boards were flooded with speculation—it could be tonight at 3 a.m. EST! It could be next week! And W.A.S.T.E. presale tickets, in addition to allowing fans to bypass the horrors of the Ticketmaster general onsale, were also generally the better seats in the house (including the orchestra pit at the very feet of Yorke and co.).[10]

And so, the only thing to do was to get up periodically and hit F5 on the saved screen opened to the "Not Yet On Sale" page of W.A.S.T.E. But that was not, in fact, the only thing to do.

The other thing to do at 3 a.m. after a ticket onsale check was to log on to the chatrooms and discuss the communal agony of waiting. To speculate about which deep cuts would be played on the tour, whether Thom would address electoral politics from the stage, what design of officially branded water bottle would signify the deepest solidarity with the band's ecological agenda (I'm not kidding). And when the onsale finally came and the fan community went into full F5 mode, competing with each other to grab tickets, the threads were the place to celebrate success and lament failure—the nerdiest post-marathon winner's circle ever. Friends and family might not get why obsessive F5

10. It's perhaps worth noting that, in what can only be interpreted as an act of mercy toward fans, the *Moon Shaped Pool* tour's fan club presale had a clearly delineated onsale date and time.

pushing meant something in those hours, but there was a community that did.

Like most Internet communication, it was diverting, sometimes acrimonious, often frivolous, but more often than not deeply connective. It was and is consumption, but it is consumption that forms a sort of odd connectivity that is no less real for being fully ephemeral and episodic.

IV

So what does this anecdote of Radiohead, the marketplace, and consumption have to do with theology and the marketplace? What can theology learn?

The church, too, can sometimes be in the habit of talking about theological authenticity as if the gospel itself is some transcendent, pure message that has to endure the necessary evil of somehow entering the rhetorical and physical "marketplace" of church competition—particularly in places such as the United States, where there is no established government preference toward one church or another. The church can act as though the marketplace is somehow accidental to, or subsequent to, and thus cheapening of the gospel.

This impulse is, on the one hand, understandable—anyone who has sat through late night televangelism can attest that church life, when it embraces the marketplace wholeheartedly and without shame, becomes horrifically cheesy and even damaging pretty quickly. This is how church becomes corporate rock—Joel Olsteen as the Nickelback of ministry. There is an inherent tendency among many theologically serious Christians—a tendency that has deep roots in Christian history—to establish an inverse relationship between scale and authenticity, an inverse relationship between power and truth.

But there is an opposite danger. We all have rolled our eyes at the stereotypical record store clerk whose tastes are so niche so as to not only strain credibility but to cut off any sort of attempt at musical community—as in the famous Venn diagram whereas the two circles "music I like" and "music you like" overlap in a space of "music I used to like!" Niche, the austere consumption of culture at a certain level of quality and obscurity (with those two often being conflated), can form community, but too much niche can harm it as well. "Indie" becomes "independent" becomes simply another word for . . . alone. This applies to niche music as much as it applies to niche church.

Wendy Fonarow identifies this dynamic of niche austerity (as it relates to music) that damages community largely in terms of nostalgia:

> Indie's nostalgic miserablism is potent in the lyrics of the Radiohead song "The Bends": "My baby's got the bends. We don't have any real friends. Just lying in a bar with my drip feed on talking to my girlfriend waiting for something to happen and I wish it was the '60s. I wish we could be happy. I wish, I wish, I wish that something would happen." . . . Indie is filled with longing for something lost or perhaps wishing for something that never was.[11]

Both in fashion and in refusal to pollute the ears (or, indeed, pollute identity?) with substandard music, the indie community's austerity tries to center-set questions of

11. Wendy Fonarow, *Empire of Dirt: The Aesthetics and Rituals of British Indie Music* (Middletown: Wesleyan University Press, 2006) 75.

who is in and who is out. But these shifts are tricky. As Fonarow goes on to ask, what defines indie anyway?

> Is it a means of distribution, a genre, an ethos, a style, or an aesthetic? . . . There is an indie ideology, but defining membership in a community by adherence to its associated ideological framework results in the inclusion of only the most fully dedicated members. However, people are far more complicated than strict definitions permit, and they participate in more than one community. Indie is located ultimately in its discourse about its boundaries, in discussions of what it is and what is not, because what it is constantly changes.[12]

And indeed, it is precisely these contestations over boundaries and purity that itself become the substance of connection. "The combination of sensitivity, discipline, intellectualism, irony, and austere modes of production expresses the pain of isolation and the belief that there was once a time when things were different. There was a time when one's sense of self was felt in an intimate fashion, when one felt connected to someone and some place. It also speaks of the hope that it can be that way again."[13]

To relate this to the earlier anecdote: AtEase fans are weird, and the bounds of real Radiohead fandom are nowhere more discussed and guarded than in that community. Derision of the jocks who come to Radiohead shows and yell for "Creep" runs legion on the threads. But again, in a world in which normal citizens with more socially acceptable fanaticisms—say, sports—cannot understand what waking up and randomly hitting F5 and then getting

12. Fonarow, *Empire of Dirt*, 77.

13. Fonarow, *Empire of Dirt*, 78.

online to talk about it might mean, shared contestation about connection can at least serve as a pretty solid stand-in for the real thing (for better or worse).

Meanwhile, anyone connected to the rhythms of contemporary church life, particularly in Europe and North America, can recognize the dynamic at play in debates between large and niche, between inclusion and purity. Theologians who write about the church tend consistently to betray a longing for a community with clear boundaries, whether that is the crisply defined orthodoxy of adherence to a set teaching authority (as in much, though not all, Roman Catholic theology) or the intensely countercultural, "single narrative" communities held together by common life and defined practices (as in contemporary anabaptist-influenced ecclesiologies). Contestations around community's boundaries, perhaps inadvertently, becomes the stuff of connection and community itself. Meanwhile, among both established and emergent Christian denominations, the impetus and ethos behind church planting often becomes an unabashed appeal to niche. Can't find a church that you want to attend? Plant the church that you would want to attend!

Niche taste meets longing for community in the religious marketplace, and the lines between what is indexed to connection to God and what is about connection to community become blurred. Fonarow makes the connection between longing for niche community and longing for access to the divine as it has played out in the history of religion explicit:

> What we find when looking at indie's discourse
> is an articulation of unresolved conflicts regarding the ritual means of accessing the numinous.
> Ideological concerns about the nature of how

one experiences the world are not confined to the domain of the sacred. Indie's non-exclusive series of definitions affirms a particular world view about how to establish an appropriate relationship between the music fan and music. Indie's support of independent ownership of the means of production and distribution, its assertions regarding the debasing influence of centralized authority, its valuing of a direct (rather than mediated) experience of music, its tropes of asceticism, introversion, autonomy, piety, simplicity, and the everyday, and its call for a return to the purity of a previous era articulate a Puritan ideology suffused with Romantic emotionalism and sensitivity. Are we to believe that this convergence of concerns and details regarding practices is merely random happenstance?[14]

Indeed, as Fonarow's extended analogy suggests, the parallels between the course of rock music and the course of Christian history center around the interplay between the aforementioned global influence or "stage" of the institutional church and various niche protest movements seeking a return to the supposed purity of a gospel uncorrupted by institutional concerns. Consider Jesus chastising the Pharisees, or the early monks fleeing into the desert in order to escape the Christianized urban setting, or Martin Luther launching theological tirades against the economic and doctrinal edifice of medieval Catholicism, or various Puritan movements escaping English establishment trappings, or "emergent" churches in our own day modifying the impulses of evangelicalism toward postmodern suspicion and doubt. To put it in Biblical terms, Jerusalem has always bred Antiochs, and Antiochs become Jerusalems.

14. Fonarow, *Empire of Dirt,* 76

Scale and niche, city and desert, cathedral and country church, Christendom and fringe have always needed each other if the gospel was to stay vital. Indeed, as with Fonarow's description of indie rock community, as often as not the very contestation of what counts as in and out, orthodoxy and heresy, quality and schlock has been central to the vitality of the Christian movement.

If scale needs to breed niche (like AtEase) in order to provide authenticity and vitality, then it is equally true that niche needs scale in order for genuine community to happen. To separate niche and scale artificially is a trick of advertising; they need each other.

V

Radiohead is a massive, corporate band and a massive, corporate brand. But it is also a force for genuine weirdness within the musical marketplace. Brad Osborne, in a masterful study of the band's compositional techniques, argues,

> Radiohead's music from 1997 onward transcends the conventions heard on *Pablo Honey* and *The Bends* by providing novel timbres, forms, rhythms, and/or harmonies in nearly every song. But in presenting these surprises within a recognizable frame (rock music), the music facilitates a fertile ecosystem for mutual interactions between listening subject and musical object.[15]

In other words—it's a musical Trojan horse. What presents itself as a straightforward rock or radio hit draws the

15. Brad Osborne, *Everything in its Right Place: Analyzing Radiohead* (Oxford: Oxford University Press, 2017) 13.

listener in and then hits her with a different sonic universe than what might have been expected. We might expand this to say that, in both its recording and also its regular large-scale tours, the band mainstreams experimental weirdness. They are a rock band who write rock songs and do rock band things. But within that familiar framework, they function to disrupt status quo standards of what is possible to get away with—and excel at—in popular music.

It's important to be precise. The claim here is not that Radiohead is among the edgiest rock bands working today; their music is downright conventional when placed alongside such sonic experimentalists as Swans, Supersilent, or Meredith Monk. Even with the move from EMI to self-released recordings, by no meaningful definition of the term is Radiohead "indie." But scale and niche are not entirely separate options; as in the history of the church, they intertwine. Scale, when done well, can breed pockets of niche connection. The jock at the show yelling for "Creep" and the pale indie kid keeping fingers crossed for the b-side "Fog (Again)" are both consuming the band, and the tangled lines of connection and experiential community at play are all the richer for being ultimately difficult to parse.

Meanwhile, as we have been seeing, Radiohead is able to curate its music and influences at a global scale. This scale means, among other things, access. For all that we might revere the obscure, "you've probably never heard of them" aesthetic of the latest indie rock sensation known only to a dwindling supply of record store clerks, the simple truth is that even in an Internet age the question of whether the majority of the population will be given access to boundary-pushing, quality music rests upon whether or not there exist bands that can embody musical risk and excellence at a certain level of popularity.

A related example might illustrate this. After the death of Nirvana frontman Kurt Cobain, his manager told the story of how the band allowed Wal-Mart to censor the cover of their album, *In Utero*, so that it could be sold in Wal-Mart and not simply hip record stores. Two thirds of the band, Kurt Cobain and Krist Novoselic, grew up in Aberdeen, WA, "and the only place they were able to get their music was Wal-Mart and Kmart," the band's spokeswoman, Janet Billig, has said. "They really want to make their music available to kids who don't have the opportunity to go to mom-and-pop stores. They feel strongly enough to make some alterations."[16]

Platforms matter. Large platforms allow bands, and churches, to at least consider what it might mean to put forward beauty instead of kitsch. Platforms are places of power to curate (such as Radiohead choosing carefully the often-edgier opening bands that it wants to introduce to its sizable audiences on tour, or Thom publicizing "office listening charts" on the band's website highlighting often obscure electronic and classical tracks with the knowledge that the lists will send fans scurrying to Spotify to learn something new). While there may be experiments that a fringe band playing to a club of 200 people can pull off, there are also aspects of connectivity that emerge in the shared experience of 10,000 in an arena or half a million listening to *King of Limbs* the moment it drops online. Complaints that Radiohead as a band is too brand-conscious miss one of the band's core achievements—to enact the gamble that genuine musical experimentalism can live in arenas, that large-scale consumption ("just keep hitting

16. Jeff Gordinier, "Discount Stores Refuse to Shelve Nirvana's Latest," *Entertainment Weekly,* April 8, 1994, http://ew.com/article/1994/04/08/discount-stores-refuse-shelve-nirvanas-latest/.

F5") can manifest community, that authenticity does not die when it leaves obscurity.

VI

So what can the church learn from Radiohead (the band and the brand) when it comes to existing in the push/pull of arena and niche of the marketplace?

The gospel is not separate from its material proclamation in concrete settings. The church is not separate from the marketplace, and for it to succumb to the temptation to present itself as somehow pure apart from its location within the realm of consumption and commerce is not only to succumb to a delusion, but to miss an opportunity. If, as I would argue, the marketplace is inevitable, then the point is not to try to hunker down and keep the gospel pure from market forces. The point is to ask, rather, within the context of a vapid global neoliberalism that commodifies beauty in order to allow its consumption to reinforce unsustainable disconnection and spiritual ennui ("all these things into position"), what it might mean to subvert the status quo by bringing the disruption to the largest platform possible. Rather than allow good music to flee from the cathedral of the arena to the desert hermitage of the small club, Radiohead embraces global stardom and uses its capital to purchase musical freedom.

Put simply, Radiohead puts the lie to the idea that authenticity and popularity are inimical, that quality means obscurity, that experimentalism and integrity must live apart from large stages and large influence. Likewise, the church needs to get over the idea that brokering capital and influence is inimical to authenticity. Yes, there are vapid and shallow megachurches in the landscape of

Christendom, just as there are vanilla and soul-deadening bands that fill arenas. Yes, there are a number of contexts in which the tiny rural congregation is doing a better job of keeping the gospel alive than the large-membership church down the street. But the phenomenon of Radiohead should hearten those who want to believe that, even in a post-Christendom west, something like authenticity and success can align. Integrity and excellence can live in multiple places within the broad marketplace of music and of religion, if Radiohead can be taken as the evidence.

Radiohead was large enough in 2007 to pioneer "pay what you want," and in so doing opened up a reorientation of how the Internet can abet music commerce outside the direct control of industry labels. Radiohead could tour in tents without corporate labels, and in so doing bring Naomi Klein's *No Logo* to a much wider audience than it would have commanded otherwise. The massive income from the band's tours allowed it to pay extraordinary amounts of money to have its light system for the *In Rainbows* tour consist of more environmentally friendly LED lighting. None of these gestures is earth-shattering, but grand. Earth-shattering gestures are not what ultimately move the chains on real transformation. Radiohead leverages its stage and its capital to move within the machine, and in so doing provides a steady heartbeat of life that thumps loudly enough to be heard across the world.

Whatever the fate of global Christendom moving forward, whatever the future of the interplay between who holds the stage and who controls the niche, the church should not try to evade the marketplace but rather creatively embrace—and perhaps subvert—the possibilities inherent in the shifting stages of modern consumption. Nothing is pure in music and nothing is pure in Christian theology. But when the event of consumption becomes the event of connection, from the global scale to the concert arena to the chat rooms and beyond, then some strange new creative currency amidst the "dollars and cents, pounds and pence" has been put into circulation.

3

"The Best You Can Is Good Enough"

The Theological Refusal of Consolation

I

For those listening to mainstream rock radio, the release of *Kid A*'s first single was a bit of a feint. Coming as the long-anticipated follow-up to the commercially successful and critically adored *OK Computer*, *Kid A*'s post-rock musical aura and abandonment of straight-ahead songwriting for electronic ambience would initially throw both critics and fans for a loop. In what can only seem in retrospect like a simultaneous appeasement and fake-out, though, the band released as *Kid A*'s first radio single the most conventional rock song on the album. As is so often the case with Radiohead, though, things were not as straightforward as they initially appeared—or, indeed, sounded.

"Optimistic," whose tenure as a radio single ended up being significantly shorter than "Karma Police" or "Paranoid Android," strikes the ear immediately in that, unlike with many other Radiohead songs, there is no lag at all between when the percussion hits and Yorke's ethereal vocal, in a wordless descant, begins. Over a murky, dropped-D tuning that lends harsh reverberation to what might be otherwise jangly guitar chords, Yorke conjures images of an absolutely graceless world of competition: "Big fish eat the little ones . . . not my problem, give me some." It is a rock song, but one that gradually opens up, not into a cathartic chorus, but an increasingly cramped lyrical and sonic space. The "hook" of "you can try the best you can / the best you can is good enough" eventually disintegrates into wordless groaning even as the guitars scrape more and more atonally against a relentless tribal backbeat. The title is revealed to be utter sarcasm, and the listener rocking out to the song has been led down a dark path—a trajectory that, as *Kid A* fans know, will only intensify throughout the second half of the album.

As is so often the case with Radiohead, the music undoes the ostensible theme of the lyrics, revealing the supposed sincerity as a sneer—the track is anything but hopeful. But perhaps this is the point. Perhaps the track can be seen as embodying one of Radiohead's signature moves—to eschew cheap "optimism" in favor of something more tentative, more fragmentary, more real. In this chapter, I want to argue that this is a crucial aspect of the power of Radiohead's music, and that refusal of ephemeral consolation allows the band to soundtrack resistance to the forces of death—all these things into position—that populate "Optimistic" and populate our world.

II

In order to set the stage for how this achievement might relate to theology proper, let's do a thought experiment.

Think, for a minute, about what images are conjured in you when you hear "Christian" applied as an adjective to a piece of pop culture art.

A "Christian" movie. "Christian" rock. "Christian" young adult novels. And so on.

What comes to mind?

Whenever I am teaching seminary courses—and note, these students tend to be committed Christians, many of whom are preparing for the ministry—I tend to pose this question. After some uncomfortable silence and/or preemptive qualifications, students tend to agree that to put "Christian" in front of art these days is to manage expectations along the following lines: the art will be wholesome, free of anything unduly offensive, and also performed less well. "Christian" rock will not have swear words, but it will be less musically innovative and interesting than "secular" rock. A "Christian" movie will not have gratuitous nudity, but it will be less cinematically complex and more moralistic than, say, a Bergman or Cohen brothers film. For the most part, "Christian" denotes safety, and safety denotes a downgrade in quality.

This is ironic on a number of fronts. For one, historically, the church was—for all its desire to repress heresy and censor what it found morally offensive—also the patron of what we now recognize as much of the outstanding artworks of our time: the Sistine Chapel, the Mass in B Minor, etc. Past art that was explicitly Christian might have been accountable to certain rules, but it was also accountable to quality. When did the label "Christian" start meaning that art would become moralistic schlock?

Theologically, an even deeper irony is that for Christians to draw strong distinctions between "sacred" and "secular" art is to miss the core event of Christian proclamation: that God in Christ becomes human, that the very world (*saeculum*) that God creates is also the world that God inhabits in fleshly terms and in so doing redeems. When it comes to art criticism and appreciation and consumption, strong distinctions between secular and sacred run the risk of being anti-incarnational.

This anti-incarnationalism presents a particular danger when it comes to how turning art "Christian" in this day and age degrades its quality: when we think of the aforementioned safe "Christian" movies and music, they tend to be pervaded with a kind of relentless cheer. Marriages are hard, but viewers can be confident that faithfulness and patience will fix them. People may die tragically, but if they are sufficiently good/pious they will go to heaven where everything will be alright. The world is okay. All these things into position.

It may very well be that, in our time, the reason why the church loses so much credibility among thoughtful people who seek beauty as well as truth is not because of the plausibility or implausibility of doctrines, but because the church is seen as a naïve purveyor of thin optimism—its own "nervous messed up marionette / floating along on a prison ship"—in the face of human tragedy that, when faced honestly, shatters any wholesome, gleaming surface of cheap hope. If this is true, then the irony deepens even further, because not only does the core event of Christian theology involve God becoming human, but it also involves this human dying as an executed criminal, shunned by both imperial and religious authorities.

Indeed, we could say that the entirety of Christian scripture—Old and New Testament—is an extended dialogue and controversy over the relationship between human action and hope, and in its most profound moments "optimism" comes in for a severe drubbing. For every book like Proverbs, in which there seems to be a strong correlation between clean living and prosperity, there are books like Job and Ecclesiastes. In Job it is in fact the righteous one who ends up surrounded by the ashes of a broken life, seemingly at the whim of divine forces inscrutable to him.[1] In Ecclesiastes the wise man looks around at his surroundings and sees the righteous suffering and the wicked prospering, with no apparent rhyme or reason to either. Scripture does not speak with one voice about the nature and grounds of hope, and it is precisely in this plurivocity that it allows the suffering to find themselves as part of the stream of debate.

Thus, while it is unfortunately true that "Christian" as an adjective has tended to become a sign that the art in question traffics in cheap hope, Christian theology has potential to complicate rather than simplify complex questions around the nature of what it means to believe that life, art, beauty, and meaning are worth pursuing, have some enduring value beyond the suffering that we endure and bring upon others.

Radiohead is, as we have said throughout, not a "Christian" band, which in the context we have been discussing is (unfortunately) likely to be a credit to the quality of their music. But they are a band whose lyrics, musicality, and aesthetic complicates questions around hope, joy, and depression. To a regularly caricatured degree, they are often thought of as a "sad" or "depressing" band—in the

---

1. It is perhaps relevant to this book, though, to note that Job 42:6, which is often translated in a way that implies that Job apologizes for his eventual outburst to God, is better translated as a mode of resignation to mystery rather than apology: Job does not "despise himself and repent in dust and ashes" but rather "comforts himself that he is dust and ashes."

director's commentary of the film *Superbad*, Jonah Hill's character's tears are impromptu attributed to the fact that "he must have been listening to Radiohead." While, as discussed in the last chapter, the band regularly headlines arenas and music festivals, the popular impression of the average Radiohead listening experience often conjures sullen, solo mouthing along to depressing lyrics while alone in a bedroom.[2] Rock listening as solipsistic navel-gazing.

But is that the whole story? If, as has been and will continue to be argued throughout this book, Radiohead's art undoes standard contrasts between such easy binaries as sacred/secular, indie/successful, etc., then one such contrast is between intense inwardness and outward activism. Music fans do not have to choose between headphones and protest lines. The two intensities can and are held together in the Radiohead phenomenon, particularly around climate change.

III

There is a strong activist streak in Radiohead's art. The band members' passions are particularly focused on global climate change. Their official artistic consultant, Stanley Donwood (whose art adorns a number of the band's album covers) regularly depicts rising sea levels swallowing whole cities. Yorke is a vegetarian, and the band has worked in a number of ways to reduce the massive carbon footprint associated with touring rock acts.

---

2. Although the strong crossover appeal of the band is evidenced in the opening lines to pop sensation Katy Perry's 2010 song, "The One that Got Away": "Summer after high school, when we first met / We made out in your Mustang to Radiohead."

Climate change is not one issue among others. The slow commodification and degradation of the earth, while ultimately threatening all of us, is also paradigmatic for how human beings commodify and discard others. The humanity of Third World farmers has to be quantified and ultimately discounted in order for current death-dealing neoliberal policies regarding oil, carbon, and unlimited economic growth to be supported. To protest on behalf of the earth is to protest on behalf of humanity, specifically the most marginalized and weakest among us.

When asked, in a 2015 interview, how his concerns about climate change are reflected in his music, Yorke responded,

> I just think these things are part of my every-day existence. I read George's articles, I read stuff that Greenpeace sends me and I guess that gets sucked into my work, but not in an obvi-ous way. The first problem is how it flows into your work and whether it has a place in your songs or whether you should just talk publically about it. I believe that any great work of art is, in itself, a form of resistance against a sense of powerlessness. The struggle against this feeling and the dissonance between our deepest feel-ings and what we are being told: these are the things that have always had a place in my lyr-ics. I am really fundamentally interested in the difference between—for want one of a better phrase—people power VS other power. I am fundamentally fascinated about the relation-ship between government and people, and those who perhaps control the way we think or try to and those who resist that. That has always been deeply fascinating to me, since I was 11 years old and read *1984*. . . .

> I don't think I'm that political. Banksy is always political. I like his work because it's implicitly or explicitly political and always slightly silly at the same time. But music is different. Music goes in phases of being completely brain dead or not. I went through a period where music was actually very political. That was when Radiohead participated in the Tibetan Freedom Concerts organized by the Beastie Boys, in 1998 and 1999. They were my heroes because they did things really independently but yet they were on a big label. The passive resistance, the way they dealt with the media . . . it was really influential.

In the same interview, Yorke dismissed the idea that the band would ever write and perform a protest song around climate change: "If I was going to write a protest song about climate change in 2015, it would be shit. It's not like one song or one piece of art or one book is going to change someone's mind."[3]

However, the following year's album *Moon Shaped Pool* would feature "The Numbers"—the most explicit and straightforward protest song in the band's career.

> We call upon the people
> The people have this power
> The numbers don't decide
> The system is a lie
> A river running dry
> The wings of butterflies

3. Yohav Oremiatzki, "Thom Yorke and George Monbiot: 'We Have to Prepare for the Inevitable Failure of COP21,'" *Télérama*, November 21, 2015, http://www.telerama.fr/monde/thom-yorke-and-george-monbiot-we-have-to-prepare-for-the-inevitable-failure-of-cop21,134497.php?utm_content=bufferde23f&utm_medium=social&utm_source=twitter.com&utm_campaign=buffer.

> And you may pour us away like soup
> Like we're pretty broken flowers
> We'll take back what is ours
> Take back what is ours

Compared to the more oblique references to global disaster in, say, *Kid A*'s "Idioteque" or the *In Rainbows Disk 2*'s "4 Minute Warning," "The Numbers" is stark in its straightforwardness. While Thom's increasing commitment to global activism around climate change has found its way into lyrics before, the decision to record and release "The Numbers" seems like an invitation from the band to ask, What does a real protest song look like? How does it fit with an aesthetic of defiance?

IV

Let's move those questions into the realm of theology, then.

How to speak about the human situation in the face of ecological degradation? How to speak about God? And can the fact that Radiohead is so resolutely glum, so resolutely centered on facing death and meaninglessness square in the eye both lyrically and musically—can that matter when it comes to how a band can create art in and into that space?

The issue could be framed as one of "soul care," provided we do not limit that to what professional clergy do. But perhaps the larger question is around care in general: care for the soul, care for the beating heart of humanity living out life's struggles in the midst of a dying planet. This could be care offered to environmental activists, specifically, or to those involved in the struggle for creation care in general. However, it also entails the larger question of how to give and receive soul encouragement and hope for all of us in the years ahead. These years will witness the irreversible effects of global climate change, loss of species diversity, and general immiseration produced by the ravages of abuse of our environment becoming more and more prominent in our global experience (hitting the poor and vulnerable in our world first, of course), and the ability to hold on to hope that allows us to continue to strive for kindness and justice so that the situation does not further deteriorate will be of concern to all of humanity. What resources can Christian soul care bring to bear on this reality?

How can we speak of hope in the face of environmental destruction in ways that are theologically responsible, scientifically accurate, and humanly sensitive? Indeed, all three of these are necessary. For instance, Christian care that is not informed by and accountable to the best science of the day can be no better than wishful thinking. Likewise, if theological speech is neither theologically acute nor humanely wise, then it cannot convey the gospel. And to be clear, that gospel (as it relates to creation and its travails) is this: that God in Christ is at work restoring all creation (Rom 8), and that Christian hope looks toward the day when all nature—including but not limited to humans—is brought into the fullness of salvation as God's "new heaven and new earth" (Rev 21:1).

Christian theology has bequeathed to us a consistent witness that Christians look for the day when God refashions the material world that God made and loves so that it participates in the fullness of life-eternal precisely as materiality. This Christian vision, elaborated by thinkers as diverse as Irenaeus and Lactantius to contemporary figures such as Joseph Sittler, Sallie McFague, and C. S.

Lewis, contrasts sharply with Christian theologies (both historical and in our own time, particularly at the level of popular piety) that portray the final stages of salvation as some kind of removal from earthly creation into an immaterial heaven.

Bible scholars have pointed out that part of the gospel itself is that God has given us the gift of being a part of God's sustaining creation, even as we wait for the day of our redemption. That being the case, then, all Christian ethics and soul care—whether engaging topics related to the environment itself or remaining only at the level of an individual's needs within that matrix of creation, suffering, and redemption—should have this gospel proclamation as the "account concerning the hope in us" (1 Pet 3:15). Moreover, as a number of ecological theologians have noted, such a worldview has the potential to provide a convincing rationale and powerful impetus to drive and orient our own efforts toward creation care now. The belief that there is SOMETHING that can be done—"the people have this power/the numbers don't decide"—is not wrong.

There is, nonetheless, another line of thinking in the Christian tradition that could be helpful in our search for resources for soul care for these times of ecological devastation and angst, and it is one where Radiohead's resolute refusal of consolation can be a guide. Theology can learn from Radiohead how to conceptualize the move from consolation to holy sadness as a theologically defensible and humane mode of environmental activism. This move, I would suggest, mirrors the very dynamic that Radiohead leverages so powerfully in its music: a refusal of consolation PRECISELY AS a soundtrack to defiant action.

V

The Christian necessity to proclaim the gospel of Christ's resurrection and creation's restoration should not eclipse the powerful resources that we have within our own tradition for naming with brutal exactitude the ways in which the forces of death to which we are subject (and of which we are often the agents) cause pain and injustice in our world. Indeed, sometimes even the feeling of guilt or sin can be a kind of psychological barricade against even greater terror in the face of seemingly random suffering or loss; as the saying goes, many of us would rather feel guilty than helpless.

A basic truth known by seasoned Christian caregivers is that the one giving care should not rush to "paper over" pain being expressed in, say, a situation of mourning with premature proclamation that all will be well because of the gospel. Heaven is not the easy solution to earth's pain; if we make it so, we are in the territory of wishful thinking so derided by Marx, Nietzsche, and Freud. While the gospel does provide a bedrock of ultimate hope, such a bedrock should not stifle people's awareness of the realities of pain and death but should rather provide a space where Christians can find the resources to be even MORE courageous than those caught in the frantic denial of mortality and pain (a denial encouraged by the rush of neoliberal capitalism's advertised promises). The same applies to the reality of despair in the face of environmental degradation

Therefore, I would contend that, while Christians certainly have a role in staving off ultimate despair (particularly the kind that leads to moral paralysis or indifference) by freely proclaiming confidence that death will not have the final word in our planet's experience, if that proclamation becomes synonymous with a Pollyana-ish naiveté about the magnitude of the ecological catastrophes that threaten human existence, the damage to the credibility of Christian claims is significant. People wanting truth would then rightly stay home from church and listen to Radiohead, all in the name of theological bullshit avoidance.

Can Christianity do better than this, better than it has often done?

A clue for another way forward—one that draws on the sort of interweaving of theology and art that we are attempting in the case of Radiohead—can be found in a concept that Orthodox theologian Peter Bouteneff outlines in relation to the music of Estonian composer Arvo Pärt—a favorite of Thom Yorke's. The octegenerian Pärt, who for the last four years has been the most performed living composer in the world, has been featured in numerous movie soundtracks and has been name-checked as an influence by many popular musicians (such as Yorke, Michael Stipe of REM, and Laurie Anderson) as well as contemporary artists such as Gerhard Richter. His influence is all the more striking given the fact that, for decades, he has been a devout Eastern Orthodox Christian who has mostly composed settings of liturgical and sacred texts. Why would an Estonian Orthodox composer who is reluctant to be in the public eye become an object of such widespread acclaim?

In *Arvo Pärt: Out of Silence*, Bouteneff argues that a key feature of Pärt's artistry (and its subsequent popularity among classical music connoisseurs as well as the broader public) is Pärt's ability to compose music that resonates with the Christian tradition's own refusal—when at its best—to let the triumph of the resurrection silence the pain of the crosses that are borne in this world (and, we might say, increasingly borne by the earth itself). Drawing on Orthodox traditions of spirituality, Bouteneff gives the name of "bright sadness" to this holding in tension of legitimate pain, on one hand, and hope for resolution, on the other. In describing the effects of Pärt's signature style of tintinnabuli ("little bells"), in which a melodic and triadic musical voice paired in strict mathematical symmetry combine in ways that allow silence ample space within the harmony itself (thus forming a kind of tension/resolution dynamic between melody, triad, and the resonances of the silence), Bouteneff makes the following observation:

> The tension and the resolution at any given moment are created by the confluence of the stable and the straying, the divine and the human. . . . [T]he divine-human relationship, in all its dimensions, is one of consonance and dissonance: divine and human are both radically other (uncreated vs. created), and also intrinsically related (the one is made in the image of the other). Construing the voices as "divine and human" will speak also to the paradox of the eternal and the engaged, the tension of time and timelessness. Contrary to the criticism of Pärt's music as sitting coldly outside of time, it is deeply embedded within it in solidarity with those who experience the vicissitudes of history. That is the melody. But it suggests timelessness in a way that both grounds the historical and indicates its upward movement. That is the triad.[4]

To continue and intensify this musical analogy as it relates to care of broken souls: it is documented that a number of patients in hospice and other critical care situations request to hear Pärt's music as they are in their care settings. Why might this be? I suspect that many of us

4. Peter Bouteneff, *Arvo Pärt: Out of Silence* (New York: SVOTS Press) 185.

have experienced hospital settings in which classical music—even otherwise excellent music—has been piped in to treacle effect: the incongruously joyous strains have the effect, not of lightening the mood as might ostensibly be their purpose, but rather to render inauthentic the voice of beauty in the face of pain. As per our discussion above, this might indeed be the function of much ostensibly "Christian" music—relentlessly cheery and relentlessly airy bullshit, floating so transcendently above pain that it dissolves into ephemera that is worse than useless. It becomes a soundtrack of otherworldliness, of irrelevance, and as such becomes simply "another thing into position." By way of contrast, Bouteneff's point is that Pärt's resonance with "bright sadness" creates a kind of holy space whereby authentic acknowledgment of pain and terror is taken up within an economy of hope that—crucially—leaves plenty of room for un-interpreted silence, for pain too deep for words.

This taking up, this humane space creation, is a mode of cultural production that allows joy because it does not impose it. It speaks to sadness because it does not try to cure it or fix it. It brings God—the Redeemer—in the spaces of silence, not of God-noise desperate to drown out cries of pain. The caregiver whose way of being in the world might embody such a stance might not come across as "cheerful" any more than does a given composition of Pärt's, or a given track on *OK Computer*. But likely such a caregiver will be the one trusted when the brittle gods of cheerfulness fail to illumine a darkening world.

We can discern a similar effect in Radiohead's music, particularly in the aforementioned tensive contrast between lyrics and vocals. Consider the fan favorite "Let Down," which exemplifies the contrast that we have highlighted repeatedly between sonic beauty and lyrical tension. Lyrically, an initial reflection on the anodyne spaces of public transport hubs ("taking off and landing / the emptiest of feelings") gives way to something more sinister ("crushed like a bug in the ground"). As Tim Footman puts it,

> "Let Down" expresses the need to avoid any corny expressions of feeling. In an effort to protect himself from the bullshit of contemporary culture, Yorke (or the narrator whose voice he adopts) must grow a shell that wards off attachment to the things that really don't matter. But his emotional protection is nothing more than the fragile carapace of an insect, and he's obliterated beneath the careless boot of capitalism. . . . The track also retains a crucial paradox of classic indie pop, in the apparent contradiction between the form (chiming, soaring guitars, expressing optimism, even triumph) and the content (lyrics about disappointment and dying insects).[5]

Tales of a crushed bug undergirded by a sonic wave that crescendos deep in the gut. We have said it multiple times and must say it again now: Radiohead juxtaposes lyrics that resist false cheer with music that presses insistently toward a beauty that holds, if not the certainty of redemption, at least the human possibility of hope.

It matters, perhaps, that to the extent that such hope is musical, it is also wordless—do not the scriptures speak of the times when we are too overcome to form words of hope ourselves, so that God's own spirit has to groan too deep for words (Romans 8:26)? As Albert Blackwell puts it,

5. Footman, *Welcome to the Machine*, 73.

Whereas vision entails interactions between our eyes and outer objects on which we focus, our organs of hearing, the middle and inner ear, are palpably more inward, their sensitivity is more omnidirectional, and their selectivity is less delineating. Thus our hearing conveys intimacy and immersion. Indeed, the sense of intimacy is even nearer. Our inner ear perceives sound not only by means of the outer ear but also from vibrations within our skull, and we feel sound, especially low frequency vibrations such as those of drums, bass organs, and large organ pipes, in our chest and abdomen. As mystical religious experience conveys immediacy and immersion in cosmic rhythm, dissonance, and harmony, music conveys immediacy and intimacy in their sonic equivalents.[6]

Radiohead's "universal sigh" ("Bloom") and the groaning of the spirit may meet precisely in the moments where the sonic event of the music draws us up from the death that surrounds us and our planet.

VI

If theology can learn from this, then such a mode of similarly authentic Christian speech—a confluence of holding space for authentic pain amidst the larger context of hope, with the latter not overriding the former in such a way as to strain legitimacy—will be crucial as the effects of ecological degradation continue to take hold in the years to come. Humanity is, by most metrics, at risk in the coming years of entering an era in which hope will be in short

6. Albert Blackwell, *The Sacred in Music* (Louisville: Westminster John Knox, 1999) 215.

supply, and no cheap or inauthentic speech toward hope will survive the rising temperatures and sea levels.

If soul care and prophetic speech are to bear witness to an ecological sensibility, then the bearing of the theologian might indeed need to be one of bright sadness—a resolute refusal to let hope in the resurrection silence creation's cry of pain in the here and now, even as the caregiver works in tune with God's Spirit to bring about the confluence of pain, hope, and silence that bears adequate witness to humanity's sin and God's forgiveness. This will not be feel-good religion or analgesic care for souls. But when done well, it may name truth and speak life in a world that awaits God's redemption.

We cannot settle for silence. In the Radiohead track "No Surprises," the narrator of the song begs for a "quiet life / a handshake with carbon monoxide." He does not wish to be disturbed, "no alarms and no surprises / silence, please." Status quo, silence, death—all these things into position. The carbon monoxide handshake thrives on the silence of Christian complacency. Silence might be holy in some contexts, but in the context of a dying planet, it can be an aid to systemic evil.[7]

But we should say more about how this embrace of bright sadness, this lyrical and sonic juxtaposition, might relate to soundtracking a theological/ecological revolution specifically. And here it matters that there is one important point of agreement among science, ecological rhetoric,

7. "There are silences of peace, and then there are silences of complacency, stasis, regulation, piety, submissiveness, secrecy, ostracism, excommunication, the status quo, a deserted town center after dark, gloomy Sunday, a gated community, suburbia, a cold church pew, people living quiet, respectable lives or suffocating under ennui, shame, embarrassment, inhibition, boredom." David Toop, *Sinister Resonance: The Mediumship of the Listener* (New York: Continuum, 2011) 219.

and Christian theology, and it can be captured by a single truism: dying is what living things do. Mortality is built into the very fabric of life, and "mortality" at its most primal level asserts not simply the fact that that which is alive *can* die, but that it *will* die.

Ecological rhetoric of conservation is haunted by the consistent testimony from various scientific disciplines that the earth cannot sustain life indefinitely. As William Stoeger points out, "From all the indications we have from the neurosciences, biology, physics, astronomy, and cosmology, death and dissolution are the final words."[8] The scenarios by which our planet might become incapable of supporting life are well-rehearsed and legion. The transformation of the sun from its current state to that of a red-giant (then white dwarf) would render the planet uninhabitable. Impacts by asteroids and comets could prove ultimately destructive. Meanwhile, the universe itself, should it follow observable patterns in evolution and dynamics, might well contract or expand indefinitely to the point where ongoing life on any planet would become impossible. Death is in the fabric of life itself. Our world will die, even apart from the fact that we happen to be actively killing it. Death is hard-wired into the universe.

Even though care for the environment is a passionate avocation for the vast majority of working scientists today, the simple truth is that these hard-nosed scientific facts about the ultimate mortality of the earth provide little aid and comfort to ecology. This is partly because global environmentalism in particular has, from its inception, emphasized the rhetoric of "conservation." For instance, one

8. William Stoeger, "Scientific Accounts of Ultimate Catastrophes in Our Life-Bearing Universe," in *The End of the World and the Ends of God: Science and Theology on Eschatology*, edited by John Polkinghorne and Michael Welker (Harrisburg, PA: Trinity, 2000) 19.

of the signature moments in the development of the North American ecological consciousness came with the presidency of Theodore Roosevelt, who crafted the Act for the Preservation of American Antiquities and who asserted, in his seventh annual message to Congress in 1907, that "the conservation of our natural resources and their proper use constitute the fundamental problem which underlies almost every other problem of our national life." This emphasis upon conservation, as it developed throughout the twentieth century, undergirded the thinking of ecology's most significant champions (such as Rachel Carson, Edward Abbey, and Aldo Leopold). In our own day, it seems clear that most Americans, if asked to state a rationale for such eco-friendly practices as recycling and energy-use reduction, would reply using the language of conservation and preservation: "I want the earth to be a good place for my children to live." "We need to preserve natural resources." Indeed, many of the explicit "green" causes to which Radiohead has devoted itself tend to use this rhetoric, and there is no denying that it has a fair amount of power. It also tends to be relentlessly sunny and aesthetically "green" in a doe-eyed sense.

But what happens to this language of conservation when it encounters clear-eyed assessments of the earth's mortality—or, put another way, what happens when the unrelenting refusal of cheap consolation characteristic of Radiohead's music meets calls to action? If dying is what living things do, including the living planet, then why care for creation? Doesn't resignation breed apathy?

This is, I would suggest, not simply an academic question. It is an existential one, and indeed an aesthetic one as well. Those who work in ecological activism have an intimate awareness of the fact that maintaining hope and avoiding burnout in this work is difficult. The deadliest enemy of action is the temptation to conclude that efforts on behalf of the environment, however successful in the short term, are finally futile. If such despair often arises in the face of the sheer magnitude of the environmental challenges facing our world (and the corresponding magnitude of many people's unwillingness to admit that these challenges exist), then an even more fundamental threat to ecological activism might accompany honest assessment of the earth's finite capacity to sustain life.[9] Eat, drink, and be merry (and burn as much coal as possible), for in the end all will die. As Ernest Becker pointed out in his classic *The Denial of Death*, the fact that we are haunted by mortality tends to drive us toward more and more frenetic activity with less and less existential joy. The philosopher George Batailles referred to this as our endless tendency to engage in "projects," tasks that give us increasingly tenuous meaning against the backdrop of the abyss.

But if Christian theology joins ecology and science at this precise intersection—the intersection where the rhetoric of "conservation" fails in the face of the earth's mortality—then what new possibilities emerge? What happens when death is faced head on in theology and conservation as it is in the aesthetics of defiance characteristic of Radiohead?

The cheap and easy way to bring theology into environmental discussions is to use theology to "solve" science, and thus the facile, easy, and thoroughly unsatisfactory solution here would be to invoke Christian hope in the resurrection in such a way as to eliminate the pathos of the earth's mortality. This is the cheap consolation mentioned

9. See Panu Pihkala "Environmental Education after Sustainability: Hope in the Midst of Tragedy," *Global Discourse* 7.1 (2017) 109–27.

above. Now again, it is true that the Christian scriptural witness testifies to the hope that all things, including a "new heaven and new earth," will find renewal when the fullness of God's Kingdom arrives. However, it is equally true that every Christian ought to know that using hope in resurrection to deny the reality of mortality misses something essential about the human condition in the face of death. Easter might transcend Good Friday, but it does not eliminate it. This means that any simplistic attempt to shore up Christian enthusiasm for ecological "conservation" by allowing Christians to ignore science's testimony to the earth's mortality fails, and it fails not only on scientific and ecological grounds, but on Christian grounds as well.

A far more promising approach would be to ask whether Christian styles of thinking, when grounded in unsentimental acknowledgment of the earth's ultimate death, might offer to ecological ethics a more evocative and authentic way of thinking about care for creation. The most distinctively Christian contribution on that front would be to press the issue to its full extent and assert that every act of care is an act not of conservation, but of care for the dying. *Every act of care is an act of care for the dying*, and this applies as much to the earth and its creatures as it does to the various people for whom we care (and to whom we must one day say goodbye). All things are "crushed like a bug in the ground," and no amount of magical thinking can change this.

At stake here is the distinction between optimism and genuine hope—a distinction that we will have occasion to revisit throughout the rest of this book. Optimism, exposed by Radiohead as chimerical and cynical, is the belief that things will get better based on current evidence—the belief that the status quo is trending toward the positive. Conversely, hope, in theological terms, is the gritty eruption of life-giving possibilities into a situation where no grounds for optimism can be found.

To conceive of every act of care as care for the dying suggests a definitive style of understanding how and why "care" happens. In Jesus' Parable of the Good Samaritan (Luke 10:29–37), the man on the side of the road who is rescued by the Samaritan is not rescued into immortality. He is mortal, and he will die—presumably not from the wounds sustained during his beating (since he has been cared for), but from some other cause at some other time. The act of care given by the Good Samaritan is an act of care for the dying, but it is an act of care that affirms the value of life even in the face of that life's inevitable end.

Even more significant is the account of the women who bring spices to Jesus' tomb to anoint him following his crucifixion and entombment. This is an act of care for one who has died, which, as Kierkegaard reminds us, has a certain unique purity in that it is precisely an act that cannot be reciprocated. This kind of care is given in the depths of the effects of mortality, where resurrection occurs—not as a cheap evasion of death or mortality's gravity, but as a divine act of rebellion against death's reality. The women's care for the dead Jesus creates a space in which resurrection becomes, not a possibility (for resurrection as such is never "possible"), but a salvific act of overcoming on God's part. Such spaces cannot be summoned, or manipulated, or even reproduced at will. But they can occur. They are not cheap consolations of the afterlife that somehow flatten the pain of death in the here and now—they are gestures from dying hands that trace the arc of resurrection's possibility.

67

And this is why considering every act of care as an act of care for the dying has profound significance for a life lived in commitment to theological truth. It is to renounce control over outcomes. It is to refuse to tie the value of an act of care—whether for a child, a tree, or an ocean—to its efficacy in conserving the cared-for thing. It is to celebrate care for its own sake, and for the sake of the possibility that the act of care might be the occasion for the creation of resurrection space. To relinquish "conservation" in favor of "care for the dying" is to acknowledge reality as we know it, but also to honor the hope that the reality that we know might not be "the final word" at all. Naming death as reality opens up space for resurrection as God's possibility.

VII

If the framework offered above—one that puts the bleak acknowledgment of death at the center of care, one that eschews the bright aesthetics of implausible optimism in favor of the grimmer aesthetic of improbable hope— is at all true to Radiohead's art, then we can see how the experience of this sort of music soundtracking calls to action might teach theology what it means to keep Christian activism theologically grounded in the gritty truth of life, death, and redemption rather than the airy consolation that becomes yet another distracting weapon in the forces of death's arsenal. "All these things into position"—only theology grounded in honesty can knock God-talk, or hope-talk, out of position and into a space of life's revolt against death.

In the spoken-word *OK Computer* track "Fitter Happier," the computerized narrator's voice chronicles the slow breakdown of the status quo narratives of health and flourishing that fuel systemic death. "Fitter, happier, more productive . . . not drinking too much . . . eating well . . . will not cry in public . . . concerned, but powerless . . . calm, fitter, healthier, more productive, a pig in a cage on antibiotics." As in "No Surprises," the overall image is clear—the status quo of daily productivity, the positionality and the metrics of success, are slow killers of bodies, planets, and perhaps even souls. To speak honestly of this is to engage in what Burke Gertenschlager calls "bleak theology," "a theology of loss, lamentation, and elegy" that eschews cheap joy in favor of visits to real tombs—tombs where God can act on behalf of life to the extent that God so chooses (and seems to so choose).[10]

It is, I suggest, no mystery why Radiohead's appeals for action on behalf of the planet and the people crushed by its degradation take on a particular power in the context of the band's entire catalogue. It is an earned earnestness, a bracing dropping of irony and indirection in the context of a musical career that has done more justice to the bleakness of much modern living than any other band. When death is given its due, the defiance that "screams as it fights for life" brings bodies to picket lines like spices to tombs.

10. "About Bleak Theology," http://www.bleaktheology.com/about-bleak-theology/.

4

Radiohead and Salvation

I

Is there salvation for Radiohead? Can there be a Radiohead Christology? Radiohead obviously does not HAVE a Christology, but can its music evoke one? If theology insists that salvation has a Christic shape, then what is the shape of salvation if Radiohead is its soundtrack?

Thus far, we have considered how Radiohead's aesthetics of defiance might offset the tendency of religion to traffic in callow optimism rather than the hope that stems from honest engagement with the world's brokenness. Any time Christian theology talks about sin and redemption, brokenness and wholeness, the shape of that salvation is going to raise the question of Christology. But again, Radiohead is not a "Christian" band—there is no explicit Jesus or salvation anywhere in the lyrics. But are lyrics devoid of "J-count," to quote the metric used by Christian contemporary radio (that is, the number of explicit references to Jesus in a song), necessarily devoid of christological significance?

The answer is no, such music does not have to be devoid, and might perhaps be all the more christologically profound for proposing ostensible absence (more on this below). For instance, we might think of David Lang's 2008 Pulitzer-prize winning libretto, *The Little Match Stick Girl Passion*. An adaptation of Hans Christian Andersen's 1845 tale of a poor young girl selling matches in the street at Christmastime and eventually freezing to death, the piece ingeniously weaves Andersen's narrative in with snippets of various classical pieces portraying the passion of Jesus Christ. The tale itself becomes a passio, a stations of the cross. The girl becomes the Christ figure, and the moral equation of the suffering of Jesus with the suffering of the poor does not stand as a profanation of the "sacred" in Jesus—it stands, as the early church fathers would insist, as a testament that in Christ the lines between God and humanity, between human and divine suffering, blur to where spaces of crucifixion become laden with christological significance regardless of whether they are also spaces of formal religion. As with Arvo Pärt's "bright sadness" discussed in the last chapter and as is, I believe, the case with Radiohead, the event of the music becomes an event of divine kenosis that holds space for human frailty within the orbit of divine care, and it is held there as brokenness without any glossing over the depths of suffering (because to diminish the depths of suffering is to fail to take the full measure of the miracle of redemption when it happens).

In what follows, I want to get at the question of art and christological significance by thinking with the German theologian Dietrich Bonhoeffer in conversation with Radiohead's music, but also another piece of popular art—the film *Calvary*. Taken together, these three sources can help us ask (and perhaps preliminarily answer) the question, How can religion, and the Christian faith specifically, be a motivation to go deeper into the world as the world rather than an aesthetic escape from it? And can popular art be a vehicle for embodying this vision? And what does that vision ultimately have to do with salvation in Christ?

II

In Hollywood film, any time a given clergyperson is introduced as a pious individual, contemporary skepticism has trained viewers to expect that one of two things will happen: the pastor will either turn out to be corrupt and hypocritical (sexually lascivious, secretly unbelieving, financially malfeasant) or will be sidelined as irrelevant to the real "human" action of the film. Thus, viewers justifiably assume that genuine piety is either irrelevant to reality (a sort of airy, transcendent, black and white "religion" that has little bearing on the ambiguities of concrete lived experience) or that the face of genuine religious observance is a mask that hides a dark, disappointing core. Few and far between are portrayals of clergy whose religion drives them deeper into the ambiguities and broken areas of the world rather than causing them to float above them. And even when clergy are present amidst these broken areas, they are rarely there as salvific rather than villainous presences. Organized religion tends not to fare well outside the artistic treacle described in the last chapter.

The 2014 film *Calvary* (written and directed by John Michael McDonah), in its script, cinematography, and actors' performances seems aware of this deep cynicism on the part of its audience, and indeed trades on it to powerful artistic effect. This is a film that operates at several meta-layers as regards the spiritual capital of priests both in the movie's setting in contemporary Ireland (where the Catholic Church has lost significant cultural influence due to the clergy sex abuse scandals, which feature prominently in the film) and in the public imagination more broadly. It is a film that embodies ambiguity about whether even good priests in the twenty-first century ought to command any level of spiritual respect by virtue of their office. And, like Radiohead's music, it does this from a somber and grim aesthetic that makes any hints of redemption seem fragile and hard won.

The film begins with a graphic verbal scene in a confessional, where an unseen man tells Father James (Gleeson) that he was sexually abused as a child by a priest, and as a result he plans to kill James at the beach the next Sunday. Intriguingly, the killer targets James precisely because the man thinks he is a good priest; whereas the death of a bad priest would be no harm to the church, the murder of a good priest would be significant revenge. He tells James that he will be murdered in a week (James knows the parishioner's identity, but it is kept from the audience until the end of the film).

James proceeds to go about his pastoral duties, counseling the cynical people in his small village (including his own suicidal daughter from his marriage prior to entering the priesthood) in gritty situations. Spousal abuse, chronic infidelity, assisted suicide, and the malaise of a millionaire occupy James's attention; there is even a disconcerting series of conversations with a former confirmation student in prison who has become a cannibalistic serial killer. He also witnesses the faith of a young wife who has lost her husband in an accident, a faith that seems supernaturally calm compared to the ambiguous spiritual negotiations happening throughout the rest of the film.

That night, James witnesses the burning down of his church. He also finds his dog dead, with its throat cut. The film drives home the generalized suspicion of Catholic clergy post-sex abuse scandal when, while walking down a country lane, James chats with a young girl whose father drives up and angrily snatches her away, verbally wondering if James had sinister motives. At this point the film takes an even darker turn: at the pub, an atheist village doctor tells James a horrific story about a small child rendered deaf, mute, paralyzed, and blind after incorrectly administered anesthesia, and contemplates aloud the theodicy issues involved in the intense suffering of a child. James, a recovering alcoholic, falls off the wagon in response and gets into a brawl with several villagers. Ashamed, James then decides to abandon the cruel village by flying to Dublin, but meeting the widow from earlier in the film and encountering her faith changes his mind. He returns to the village, reconciles with his daughter, and is murdered on the beach by the distraught parishioner (a butcher named Jack who has been a character in the film all along).

The murder scene is its own kind of crucifixion. Jack, hearing that James shed tears over his dog, asks if he cried similarly over news reports concerning children abused by priests. James says no, he had felt detached from such stories—whereupon the enraged Jack shoots James in the side and tells him to say his prayers. When James says he already has, Jack delivers a final gunshot to the priest's head. The coda to the film shows the parishioners going about their lives more or less unchanged, with the exception of Fiona, the priest's daughter, who visits her father's killer in prison in a scene echoing her father's exhortations toward forgiveness.

Throughout the film, the question of whether Father James merits the label "good" applied to him throughout the film—sometimes sincerely, sometimes sneeringly—is raised again and again. If goodness is defined by salt-of-the-earth authenticity and care of souls in the face of adversity, then James seems to be genuinely good. However, he is also an alcoholic, a largely absent father, and given to temper. More to the point, he is the moral and spiritual representative of a church whose behavior in its own scandals has left the villagers utterly unconvinced that it has the spiritual authority to censor them in their own vices. The film seems to pose the question starkly: if the church is no longer good, then can a good priest also be a good human being? This is, as we will see, a question that bothered Bonhoeffer as well.

III

One way of posing the question theologically, to borrow terms from Vítor Westhelle, has to do with issues of representation and ecclesiology in the film. Is Father James's complex character meant to be a portrait of the church in its messiness? A human proxy for Christ, or Christ's body?[1] Or does the film participate in the contemporary suspicion that somehow genuine religious piety and authentic human struggle are cinematically at odds?

If representation involves issues of how the church is imaged, and if the theological question at stake in the representation of the church in a figure like Father James is a fundamentally christological one (how is the church the body of Christ in such cross-bearing circumstances), then we can be helped by theologians who remind us that, in theology as in ecclesiology, the image must contain its own negation in order to avoid becoming an idol. We have

1. Vítor Westhelle, *The Church Event: Call and Challenge of a Church Protestant* (Minneapolis: Fortress, 2010).

seen already how a similar tension haunts rock stars at the scale of Radiohead: to offer authentic art in the marketplace is to walk the tension between stardom capable of wielding a global platform on the one hand and negation of the rock idol bullshit in the name of artistic authenticity on the other.

For instance, as Natalie Carnes has argued in her recent book *Image and Presence: A Christological Reflection on Iconoclasm and Iconophilia*, "Without iconoclasm, iconophilia risks idolatry. Without iconophilia, iconoclasm turns to despair."[2] Theologians have long argued that God-talk needs to contain its own qualifications, its own inherent cautions against limitations, in order not to turn theological concepts into conceptual idolatry. Carnes applies this same caution to images (including the sort of cinematic imagery at play in *Calvary*) rather than words, and in so doing takes the argument one step further: iconoclasm (the impulse to combat images, religious or otherwise) contains within itself the seeds of iconophilia, love of these images; meanwhile, iconophilia needs to encompass modes of critical suspicion of what images can and cannot do (iconoclasm) if the images are not to become idols. "The negation at the heart of imaging is not an eradication nor an erasure. Neither is it a degradation of the image. It is a breaking open that leads to greater revelation. It is a way of saying that images mediate presence-in-absence and likeness-in-unlikeness."[3]

If, as I am suggesting, *Calvary* acts as a kind of cinematic meta-commentary upon our suspicions of religion even as the film engages in a searching christological

2. Natalie Carnes, *Image and Presence: A Christological Reflection on Iconoclasm and Iconophilia* (Stanford: Stanford University Press, 2017) 183.

3. Carnes, *Image and Presence*, 7

exploration of how the church does and does not repre-
sent Christ, then Carnes's framework here is helpful. In
contrast to the naïve tendency to contrast holiness and
worldliness, to place them on opposite ends of a spectrum,
a truly christological understanding of how the empirical
Christian church embodies Christ (and thus how priests
embody humanity) would hold them in hypostatic tension—exactly the sort of tension that we find in great art
and in great theology.[4]

4. As philosopher and theologian Karmen MacKendrick writes,
When we attend to speaking, even in reading, we must recognize the places where it stops and breaks. We recognize
that silence separates meaning from a pure rush of sound,
and that what is most meaningful might also be the most
elusive. We attend to music as something other than a topic,
and to the poetics of language even when it plods. The gaps
in speaking and meaning provide an avid philosopher with
places to interrupt, even to dismantle an argument. Attentive hearing without grasping, without immediately seeking
a firm control over the material, requires instead a kind
of hospitality, a giving of space to speaking. Perhaps, for
example, those gaps are not errors, but paradoxes, pulls of
tension that sustain our delight. Perhaps they are wounds:
to be healed or comforted, or to be astonishingly celebrated,
as in the gaps in Christ's side, the swords through Mary's
heart. Maybe they are gaps in memory, pulling us inexpli-
cably back. Maybe they are the memories of gaps: scars left
on the glorified, or the mimesis of the stigmata. Maybe they
are invitations: you may enter here; or: this is a conversation
space. Maybe they are the spaces through which we lose
ourselves. Maybe they are the spots where the smoothness
of time and space unfurling has given way to the disruptive
jolt of enchantment or terror. Maybe they are those spaces
in which language resonates, giving meaning to voice.

The willingness to dwell in those strange discursive
places where theology happens requires a willingness to
hear differently, to accept that language is doing something (rather than nothing) even as it struggles with its fall
into silence. Into silence, and also into sound: wondering
about saying requires attending to those who say, including the very strange (such as gods who somehow make by

This was the preoccupation, for instance, of the great theologian of christological protest Bonhoeffer, whose trajectory on this front provides a helpful framework for thinking both about *Calvary* and about Radiohead. Bonhoeffer's theological preoccupations were centered around the ambiguities of discipleship in the modern world, a world that was quickly falling into political and religious chaos around him.[5] As a Lutheran theologian, he was keen to point out that many of the most character-istically Protestant ways of reading Jesus' instructions in the Sermon on the Mount had the hermeneutical effect of reducing the force of those commands into a more general system of "ethics"—and indeed, ethics that could easily be evacuated of any critical content over and against the prevailing wisdom of the day. In his early public works, most notably *Discipleship* and *Life Together*, Bonhoeffer is at pains to highlight the contrast between the life lived in response to the call of Jesus (that is, life lived in Christian community) and the life that is blessed by the bourgeoise Christian ethics of the day—a preoccupation not unlike that faced by Father James over against his nominally Catholic parishioners.

---

speaking) and the abjectly marginalized (such as criminals nailed up to die by suffocation); to the water in water move-ments of other animals; to the world itself, which might sign or sing or cry out; to citation as it edges into recita-tion as that in turn edges into liturgy, with its deliberately contagious quoting. If there is faith in theology, it is faith that we are not speaking mere nonsense, faith that there is something here worth listening to. That something is a very abstract something most of the time. But it is a very concrete something, too. It resounds. (*The Matter of Voice: Sensual Soundings* [New York: Fordham, 2016] 127–28).

5. For elaboration of the following account of Bonhoeffer's de-velopment, see Saler, *Theologia Crucis*.

Bonhoeffer's initial theological training occurred in a context that had largely shorn Christian preaching and biblical hermeneutics of any particular apocalyptic content. It instead emphasized the coherence of Christian ethics with cultural myths of human and societal progress. This was known as "liberalism," here not meaning political progressivism but rather the attempt to reconcile Christian truth claims with the common wisdom of the age. However, under the influence of theologian Karl Barth and his own ongoing mediation on the Sermon on the Mount, Bonhoeffer gradually came to emphasize the contrastive character of Christian discipleship over and against the wisdom of the world. This narrative, which has since been appropriated by a number of Bonhoeffer interpreters, posits that the church's loss of solid theological content in favor of bourgeoise ethics of good citizenship left these ethics vulnerable to co-optation by the Nazis. Bonhoeffer's reactions against classical Protestant liberalism had at their heart the suspicion that this theological strand's anemically "ethical" renderings of the oddness of discipleship was insufficient to form communities capable of resisting fascism. Like the mute citizens of Radiohead's "Burn the Witch," the German Christians had learned to "stay in the shadows / cheer the gallows" while "avoiding all eye contact."

By the time he wrote *Ethics* and his *Letters and Papers from Prison*, however, Bonhoeffer had further nuanced his sense of the relationship between discipleship and the world, and he did so in rigorously christological terms. No longer content to focus only on the ways in which Christians are called to distinguish themselves from the world, Bonhoeffer began developing a sense that the life of discipleship calls Christians to go as deeply into the world as God does in Jesus—that is, to engage in a kind of deep incarnational sensibility. This dovetailed, biographically, with his growing involvement with the plot against Hitler, such that the theological question that came to dominate Bonhoeffer's life and work might be framed (in radical terms) as follows: if discipleship is less about keeping oneself morally and theologically pure and more about following the living Christ deeply into the ambiguities of the world qua world, then can the call to discipleship actually be a call to transgression, to sin? One here recalls Father James deciding whether or not to provide a gun to an elderly parishioner who is contemplating euthanasia—can sin be mercy, or virtue, in a world so deeply broken?

For Bonhoeffer this question of political engagement in a world of shit and chaos is heightened in impact when we realize that, while he certainly was intelligent enough to frame his decision to participate in violence against Hitler in terms of Christian just war theory or some other "ethical" form of justification, he resolutely refused to do so. Instead, in much more evocative terms, he experimented with the notion that to act responsibly in the world is to become guilty, and that such response to the world in its ambiguity is precisely an incarnational, christological gesture. At its most extreme, the question might be formulated thus: Can following Christ deep into the broken world lead us, for Christ's beloved world's sake, into sin? Can following be a following into (and unto) guilt? At the time of Bonhoeffer's execution by the Nazis for his participation in the plot against Hitler's life, it seems clear that he was working on a theological vision of christological openness to the world, in which established boundaries between sacred and profane, church and saeculum would be rendered christologically moot. Another way of putting it would be: Bonhoeffer was envisioning a radical incarnational logic whereby the church would love the world more than the world loves itself, and that such a love is itself the overcoming of any theological barrier between church and world. Such a move would go beyond "ethics" as a disembodied system of Christian formalist purity and toward the vitality of transgressive discipleship, one which makes the Christian vulnerable to the horizon of the neighbor's need in a manner that eschews purity for connection and genuine service—the Christian, like Christ, as the "man for others" (one of Bonhoeffer's favorite phrases for Jesus).

And as with *Calvary*, Christology here bleeds into ecclesiology. One of the most pathos-laden aspects of Bonhoeffer's theology is that, while he was one of the most pro-church theologians of the twentieth century, in a very real sense he was ecclesially homeless. Having grown up in a household that rarely attended church, it was only when he was traveling in Rome and caught a vision of a church that was truly "catholic" in the broad sense that his imagination was fired—an imagination that would soon find what it was looking for in the politically activated, deeply pious, black liberation theology of Abyssinian Baptist Church. However, while Bonhoeffer would carry the impressions made on him by these various experiences throughout his life, and use them both as the basis of the formation of his neo-monastic seminary experiment at Finkenwalde as well as his growing theology of resistance against the Third Reich, for the most part he experienced the church as a failure. Not only was the German church united under Nazification, but even the anti-Nazi Confessing Church movement of which Bonhoeffer was an early and enthusiastic supporter eventually disintegrated once the Nazis granted some basic concessions. His experiences running an illegal seminary at Finkenwalde, as well as his largely successful stints as a youth pastor, gave him some tastes of what ecclesial existence might look like; however, for the most part, Bonhoeffer's theology largely outpaced any existing ecclesial arrangements in his time. His church, no less than Father James, was a failure in its time and setting. To quote Thom's lyrics in "Bishop's Robes," the Nazified national church scene in Germany indeed was "Children taught to kill / To tear themselves to bits on playing fields / Dressed in bishop's robes."

This is reflected in Bonhoerffer's *Letters and Papers from Prison* when he begins to draw conclusions concerning the concrete implications of his speculations about a "world come of age." Toward the end of that text, Bonhoeffer argues that the church of the future would become less of a bourgeoise institution—pastors would live off of free-will offerings and/or be bivocational, the church would fully disestablish itself from the secular government, etc. While in some ways this simply points to the "free church" scene that would come to fruition in the United States and elsewhere, it is clear that, when taken within the sweep of Bonhoeffer's ecclesiological writings, what he is envisioning is a church that can take the same sort of incarnational risks on behalf of the world that he envisions in individuals.[6]

IV

So Bonhoeffer's thinking evolved and changed, but his focus on community stayed steady throughout. In his earlier works, he is interested in how discipleship in Christ

6. See Barry Harvey, *Taking Hold of the Real: Dietrich Bonhoeffer and the Profound Worldliness of Christianity* (Eugene, OR: Cascade, 2015).

establishes the church as a community set apart within the world for the sake of the world, one in which the call to obedience in Christ provides an apocalyptic counterpoint to the denatured Christian ethics bequeathed by liberalism. One thinks of the faith of the widow in *Calvary*, serene and transcendent in the face of tragedy and death. It is religion as courage, but also, perhaps, as projected supplement and panacea—Marx's opiate of the people. However, as his theological project continues and matures, and as his own experiments in radical ecclesiology continue, Bonhoeffer becomes fascinated with what it would mean for the path of discipleship to engage a "world come of age" by becoming more wordly than the world, more secular than the saeculum, precisely because this is what the God of weakness chooses to do in the incarnation and the crucifixion. Can the church, as a community whose actions take on less the character of public religion and more the disciplines of worship and genuine community that forms the disciple of Christ apart from institutional respectability, break free of its role as underwriter of social "ethics" and enter into the world's brokenness in weakness and in service?

Calvary raises questions about the relationship between deep engagement with—and even participation in—the world's brokenness precisely as a christological/religious act in a manner similar to Bonhoeffer, and does so in smartly self-aware fashion. However, its success as a film also stems from the fact that it does not give answers in didactic fashion—the tensions at play do not resolve. It is unclear in the end whether the death of Father James has been even remotely salvific for anyone—the tableaux of the village in the end remains one of damnation. However, the hints of forgiveness evinced by James's daughter speaking with his killer portrays what theologians have often termed the "weak" power of the cross, of Calvary itself—God is at work in the damnation, effecting salvation not by force but by gentle disruption of the cycles of violence and emptiness that comprise the status quo of our existences. As with the music of Radiohead, the film offers no easy answers as to what redemption in the world looks like. It is concerned with whether the heart can still beat inside the domino effect of brokenness that surrounds Father James and his people—the heart in the machine.

If that is the Christ that is at work in Calvary, then it is indeed fitting that James is the priest of Christ's church. His is a presence that refuses—both by choice and by lack of capacity to do otherwise—to absent himself from the world; he chooses to love the world, by gritty and abiding presence, in its most broken places. As the high priest of a church that has failed, he becomes a priest for God's own damned world—the world no more beyond redemption than anything where God's broken presence in the cross still abides. *Calvary* thus stands both as meditation and as call to the church to embrace its own failure, its own brokenness, and to engage in levels of solidarity with the world that can only be outdone by God in Christ. As Bonhoeffer might say, it is impossible to love the world more than God does; only through the way of the cross can Christ's own body, the church, go as deeply into the world as God already is. Therein lies the stations that lead to death, but also to the hope that overcomes tombs.

V

But we should interrogate this notion of "hope," since this will tie together the vision of Bonhoeffer outlined above and the aesthetic resistance rock of Radiohead. I argued in the last chapter that Radiohead's music is an antidote to optimism; however, is it also an antidote to hope? Theologian and ethicist Miguel Del Torre has written provocatively that even discourse of "hope" is a religious imposition upon reality that benefits the privileged:

> Hope, as a middle-class privilege, soothes the conscience of those complicit with oppressive structures, lulling them to do nothing except look forward to a salvific future where every wrong will be righted and every tear wiped away, while numbing themselves to the pain of those oppressed, lest that pain motivate them to take radical action. Hope is possible when privilege allows for a future.[7]

But does this need to be the final word on hope?

Here I would posit, picking up on threads above, that Radiohead's music itself stands as the kind of juxtaposition that we see in *Calvary*'s christological joining of brokenness and gritty hope, in the Chalcedonian logic of a God that saves by becoming more human than we are.

A paradigmatic instance of how this is enacted in Radiohead's music is the track "Paranoid Android," whose radical shifts in instrumentation and time signature are modeled after the Beatles' "Happiness is a Warm Gun." The song's lyrics once again evoke a now-familiar world of stultifying neoliberal "normalcy": "Ambition makes you look pretty ugly / kicking squealing Gucci little piggy." As the song's acoustic intro sections track with the narrator's growing frustrations, a remarkably abrasive three-guitar attack from Jonny, Ed, and Thom kicks in—"why don't you

---

7. Miguel A. De La Torre, *Embracing Hopelessness* (Minneapolis: Fortress, 2017) 5.

remember my name!" Then, as that section reaches fever pitch, the cadence abruptly changes again—this time into a downtempo, multi-tracked Thom falsetto that evokes choirs of angels: "Rain down . . . rain down . . . from a great height." The invocation of some numinous, some divine, seems unmistakable (the song's video features a highly ironic cartoon angel at this point). As the band behind Yorke continues to whisper of modern banalities ("pigskins . . . yuppies networking . . . "), Yorke continues to invoke the rain until he reaches one of the very few mentions of God in the Radiohead catalogue: "God loves his children, God loves his children," followed by a sarcastic "yeah" (the line apparently originally was "God loves his children / that's why he kills them"). At which point, the guitars kick in again and the song ends in an intense pedal-driven guitar fury. The message seems clear—just as the listener is lulled into thinking that the solution to modern lethal banality is some heavenly escape ("rain down from a great height"), the name of God is invoked only to end in sarcasm, and the listener is plunged into scraping electronic chaos even more intense than before.

However cathartic the ending, it seems to leave no more room for redemption than does the body of Father James lying on the beach. But here again—what is power? Is power the ham-handed and implausible assurance that somehow we can stay in the angelic clouds when the real action of the world is amidst the swirl of chaos and beauty, the crunch of machines (electric guitars) and the squall of defiant dissonance? Or is a more adequately incarnational understanding that Christ is amidst the squall, in the "weak" power of forgiveness between a daughter and her father's killer and the brief connectivity across screaming fans and screaming guitars?

VI

As "Paranoid Android" makes clear, there is no God from the machine in Radiohead. Jesus does not float down "from a great height" in Radiohead's music. But is such a Jesus what we would want anyway? When Jesus ascends into heaven at the beginning of the book of Acts, his disciples are left gaping at the sky. As Vitor Westhelle remarks,

> So let us remember the first lesson that the followers of Jesus had to learn after Jesus left them. The very first lesson was not for them to know when Jesus would return. After all he said he would be always with them to the end of the ages. How could they know that when in his ascension they were gazing up into the skies? The question was one of the gaze. So let us learn the first lesson that the disciples had to learn when the master they loved was lifted away from them. There they were standing in utter bewilderment, gazing at the clouds on high, gaping at the skies, probably wondering about his last words that said it was not their business to know about the time reconciliation would happen. Now that the master was gone from their sight they had to learn where to turn their vision to. Not when but where does Jesus return was the point. Where should the gaze be fixed at? Two men stood by the disciples when they were staring up heavenwards. And they were told by the followers that theirs was the wrong quest. "Why do you stand looking into heaven?" This is what is called a rhetorical question. Those who were asking for the time of Jesus' return, were now being told that Jesus' continuing presence, his parousia, his being-there was not a question of when, but of where. The text of Acts that tells us

that Jesus' ascension is the way, the very same way he comes to us: it is always from down below. The narrative of Jesus' ascension is only a story to tell us about his descent. "This Jesus, who was taken up from you into heaven, will come in the same way as you saw him go into heaven." It is from down below that he comes. Don't look into heaven. It is from down below that glory emerges. Don't gaze up, look down. Look down where life is broken, where creation is tortured, where nature is abused. Down there in the troubles of our days lies the glory as much as it once was found in the womb of a poor peasant maid of Galilee, or lying in a manger in the midst of dung, animals, and flies.

Consider then the homeless old woman in the city street and know that Christ is there and that NATO's whole air force in all its glory is not armored as she is. So, do consider the lilies of the field, but consider as well the pollution, the waste, and the violence against which the blossoming of the most simple flower is already a triumph that beats the odds and tells a story of ascension.[8]

The Ascension, arguably, enacts a similar kind of reversal as "Paranoid Android"—the disciples, by way of their gaze, are briefly brought into the orbit of the heavens, only to be reminded that the Christ who gives the shape of salvation into which they have put their hope once optimism died on the cross does not wish to be found there. Christ will come again as the disciples saw him go up—from below. As Acts continues, it is the weak, fragile church that eventually plunges itself into the maelstrom of

---

8. Vitor Westhelle, "The Glory Down Below," *Westhelle Turf*, July 1, 2010, http://www.vitorw.com/?s=ascension.

violence and brokenness and possibility inherent in contexts across the world in order to speak truth to violently pious bullshit (Paul), to heal the abject, and even to die (Stephen).

To have Radiohead soundtrack salvation is to become attuned to the idea that salvation is a deeper plunging into the places where Christ seeks to be found, and to trust what it means to have the world as the world be the place where God chooses to "immerse in love."

5

"You Look So Tired"

Conclusion

The title of this conclusion, "you look so tired," is a lyric that comes immediately prior to the following: "help me bring down the government / they don't speak for us." When Radiohead plays this song, "No Surprises," live in concert, it is understood among their fans that that is a fully approved moment for full-throated screaming. The track, which in typical *OK Computer* fashion begins with a well-manicured picture of suburban middle-class existence that is thinly papering over an existential scream whose culmination might be suicide ("a handshake with carbon monoxide . . . quiet"), is a slower ballad dripping with ennui. Thus, the line begs interpretation. Does it hint at an eruption of fury, a revolutionary overcoming of the systemic injustices and spiritual wounds of the status quo? Is it sarcastic, a mocking of idealistic pretensions coming from a character who has long ago acclimated to the "real world?" Or does the fact that the line is delivered in the same slow, measured borderline drawl from Thom with which he asks for "a quiet life" and "a job that slowly kills you" mean that even revolutionary pretension eventually gets beaten down and sucked into the same cycles of regret and capitulation that drain life of joy? Or does the choice even have to be made on those terms?

As we have seen throughout the book, Radiohead traffics in a lyrical and sonic interplay of crushed dreams and insistent, pulsing hope. In striking moments of earned earnestness amidst suffocating irony, the band directs its defiance toward certain enemies and in favor of key causes. The line "help me bring down the government" is a kind of cipher, a kind of Rorschach test for how one understands which side of the pendulum the band might be on. Is the band gaining credibility by naming the very real fact that so often such injunctions are mere platitudes, impotent and episodic expressions of rage that are so ineffective as to be worthy of weary sarcasm? Or is the line, particularly in its ability to bring forth communal screams of solidarity from the crowd whenever uttered live, a brief irruption of fragile hope that derives its power from the deep groundedness in reality that surrounds it? Is the oscillation itself the point? The suspended space of uncertainty between resignation and hope—this is the space of theology soundtracked by Radiohead.

In this book I have argued that Radiohead's music of defiance is an instructive soundtrack to (and thus perhaps even source for) Christian theology. Specifically, I have sought to make the case that:

1. Radiohead's embrace of its role within the marketplace, up to and including its gestures of ostensible subversion, points to the ways in which churches as brokers of various kinds of cultural capital (large and small) can rethink what it means to form community around consumption. It can also empower churches to embrace their role as platforms and brokers of economic and cultural capital by seeing the navigation of

the space between stage and niche as constitutive of ministry itself.

2. Radiohead's resolute refusal of cheap optimism raises an uncomfortable indictment of much "Christian" aesthetics, and Yorke's interventions around issues such as global climate change point to how embracing mortality (rather than simple "conservation") can provide an impetus for action on behalf of the planet and its most vulnerable that is soundtracked by deep awareness of mortality as a condition of resurrection.

3. Similarly, a Radiohead-inspired understanding of the Christic shape of salvation is one that continually refuses sharp dichotomies between sacred and profane, beauty and ugliness, and instead holds them together in such a way that fragile spaces of human connectivity to God and others within the machinery of modern life become possible.

The simple truth is that Radiohead soundtracks a planet that is slowly being killed—not slowly dying, but slowly being killed. The lifestyle of the majority of Europeans and North Americans is unsustainable on a variety of environmental, social-economic, and spiritual fronts, and much of the rest of the planet is on the verge of catching up or surpassing this consumption. It seems inevitable that sustained inhabitation of, and indeed encouragement and striving after, such a way of existing in the world cannot but produce a lingering malaise in the soul—a dis-ease born of the fact that common sense is killing us. This while much of what passes as religion in these context either seeks to soothe the consciousness of the consumer through some appeal to "mindfulness," or to weakly challenge broader systems with isolated political or spiritual platitudes without engaging in searching analysis of the church's own complicity, or—in many cases—becoming an active cheerleader of the sorts of "success," "growth," "development," and "prosperity" that are destroying us and our world. It is the "Fitter Happier" machinery of modern life—all these things into position.

Radiohead offers no grand solutions to this systemic malaise nor the underlying forces of greed, fear, and weakness that (temporarily yet intractably) sustain the unsustainable. The power of their art (apart from the fact that most of their music just rocks in sonically mind-expanding ways) stems from the fact that it both embodies and fosters intelligent defiance. It juxtaposes unrelentingly grim lyrics with music that impels the blood to keep resisting, sometimes in the form of intense beats ("Idioteque") and sometimes in the slow organic beauty of an unfolding alternative world ("Fake Plastic Trees"). It's a defiance born of clear-eyed and unflinching occupation of the lethal status quo. Rock is not social analysis, but art can capture and intensify the feelings of being trapped in a systemically sinful matrix of economic, social, and religious forces in which "succeeding" on society's terms hastens the failure of the planet and its most vulnerable people. We might imagine another poet, whose economics and politics and religion "crushed him like a bug in the ground," asking us what it profits us to gain the whole world if the cost is our souls.

Christians believe that the crushed man was resurrected by the God whose power to create and sustain life is ultimately greater than our collective ability to foster death, and that this resurrection stands as a reality testifying to the same possibility for us and for all that matters in this world. In "Videotape," the singer imagines a perfect day that can be carried into the afterlife and immortalized there, despite the efforts of devils to drag it down. In "Pyramid Song," the narrator is carried, along with his lovers, into a state where there is "nothing to fear and nothing to doubt." Nothing in Radiohead amounts to full-blown resurrection, but their music's world-weariness is suffused with a slight but intractable sense that death cannot fully crush meaning, that technology cannot fully swallow the soul, that the beating heart within the machine can still live.

Index

"15 Step", 31
"4 Minute Warning", 53

A Moon Shaped Pool, 20
Abbey, Edward, 64
Abyssinian Baptist Church,
    71, 82
activist, 50
alienation, 5, 9, 29
"All I Need", 31
Amnesiac, 17, 18
Anderson, Laurie, 57
artists, 2 , 5, 11, 19, 25, 57
Arvo Pärt: Out of Silence,
    57, 59
ascension, 88, 89
AtEase, 32, 36, 39
authenticity, 6, 8, 12, 24,
    34–35, 39, 42, 75, 77

Barth, Karl, 80
Batailles, George, 65
Beatles, 86
beauty, 7, 12, 16, 21, 23, 25,
    31, 41–42, 48–49,
    59–60, 87, 92–93
Becker, Ernest, 65
Biblical, 38
Billboard, 22
Billig, Janet, 41
Bishop's Robes, 83
Blackwell, Albert, 61–62

"Bloom", 1, 9, 61
"Blow Out", 32
"Bodysnatchers", 31
Bonhoeffer, Dietrich, 72,
    76, 78–85
    Ethics, 80
    Discipleship, 79
    *Letters and Papers from
        Prison*, 80, 83
boundaries, 36, 37, 81
Bouteneff, Peter, 3–4, 57–59
bullshit, 7, 57, 59–60, 77, 90
bureaucracy, 6, 9
"Burn the Witch," 80
Bush, George W., 18

Calvary, 72, 73, 77, 79, 82,
    84–86
    Father James, 74–76, 79,
        81, 83–85, 87
capitalism, 11, 56, 80
Carnes, Natalie, 77–78
Catholicism, 38
    Roman Catholic
        theology, 37
Chalcedonian, 86
Christendom, 26–27, 39, 43
Christian theology, 5, 10,
    12–13, 26, 44,
    48–49, 54, 63, 65,
    71, 91

Index

Christianity, 11, 27, 28, 57, 83

Christology, 11, 71, 72, 76–78, 80–81, 84, 86

church, 6, 8, 10–11, 26, 28-29, 34–35, 37–40, 42–43, 47–48, 57, 63, 72, 74, 76, 78, 80–83, 85, 89, 93

climate change, 3, 6, 19, 50–54, 92

Coachella, 11, 25

Cobain, Kurt, 41

commercial, 6, 11, 15, 20, 24–25

commodification, 23–25

community, 8, 12, 23, 28–29, 33–37, 39–40, 42, 63, 79, 83, 92

Confessing Church, 82

conservation, 63–68, 92

consumption, 22, 27, 30, 32, 34–35, 41–42, 44, 48, 92

creation, 12, 54–56, 59, 62, 65–66, 68, 89

Creep, 15, 17, 36, 40

cross, 10–11, 28, 72, 76, 84–85, 89

crucifixion, 67, 72, 75, 84

Dark, David, 7

death, 3, 7–10, 12, 27, 41, 46, 51, 53, 56, 61–63, 66, 68–69, 72, 74, 84–85, 93–94

defiance, 2–3, 10, 13, 53, 66, 69, 71, 91, 93

Del Torre, Miguel, 86

despair, 9, 12, 56, 65, 77

Dettmar, Kevin J. H., 9, 10, 11

discipleship, 80, 82–84

divine, 37, 49, 58, 68, 72, 87

Donwood, Stanley, 50

Drill, 15

Dylan, Bob, 5

earth, 4–5, 10, 16, 43, 51, 54, 56–57, 63–66, 75

Easter, 66

Ecclesiastes, 48

ecclesiology, 76, 82, 84

ecological, 7, 33, 53, 55, 57, 62, 63, 64, 65, 66

economics, 25, 30, 93

EMI Records, 15, 19

environmental, 19, 53, 54, 55, 56, 65, 66, 92

Eucharist, 29

evangelicalism, 38

"Fake Plastic Trees", 10, 16, 93–94

fandom, 17, 31–32, 36

Finkenwalde, 82

"Fitter Happier", 32, 69, 93

"Fog (Again)", 40

Fonarow, Wendy, 35–39

Footman, Tim, 29, 30, 60–61

forgiveness, 62, 75, 84, 87

freedom, 42

Freud, Sigmund, 4, 56

Gertenschlager, Burke, 69

Glastonbury, 11, 21

Gnosticism, 28

God, 2, 4–6, 15, 27, 37, 47–49, 53–55, 59–60,

62, 64, 66, 68–69,
72, 77, 80, 84–88,
90, 92–93
Godrich, Nigel, 16
Good Friday, 66
gospel, 8, 11, 27, 34, 38–39,
42–43, 54–55, 56
Greenwood, Colin, 13, 15
Greenwood, Jonny, 13,
15, 31
Greif, Mark, 2–3

Hail to the Thief, 18, 26,
29, 32
heaven, 4, 9, 48, 54, 55,
66, 88
"High and Dry", 17
Hill, Lauren, 5
Hitler, Adolf, 81
hope, 6–13, 36, 48–49, 54–
56, 58–62, 65–68,
71, 85–86, 89, 91
human, 2, 6, 12, 27, 47–48,
51, 53, 57–58, 60,
66, 72–73, 76, 80,
86, 92
humanity, 62, 78

iconoclasm, 77
iconophilia, 77
"Idioteque", 32, 53, 93
immanence, 4
In Rainbows, 4, 19–21, 25,
29, 31–33, 43, 53
incarnation, 84
indie rock (music), 26,
39, 40
Internet, 18–19, 25, 30, 34,
40, 43
Irenaeus, 54

"J-count", 71
Jesus Christ, 4, 27, 72
Job, 48
Johnson, Scott, 1, 4

"Karma Police", 45
Kid A, 8, 17–19, 22, 30–32,
45–46, 53
Kierkegaard, Soren, 67
Klein, Naomi, 26, 43

Lactantius, 54
Lamar, Kendrick, 5
Leopold, Aldo, 64
"Let Down", 60
Letts, Marianne, 22–24,
28–29
Lewis, C. S., 55
liberalism, 80, 84
life, 3–4, 7–10, 16, 26, 29,
34, 37, 43, 49, 53–
54, 62–65, 67–70,
79–82, 89, 91–93
"Like Spinning Plates", 17,
18
Lollapalooza, 11, 21
"Lotus Flower", 20
"Lucky", 2, 4
Luther, Martin, 38

machinery, 2, 8, 92, 93
machines, 11, 87
marginalized, 51, 79
marketplace, 6, 21–23, 25,
27, 29, 34, 37, 39,
42–43, 77, 91
Marx, Karl, 4, 56, 84
McFague, Sallie, 55
Meeting People Is Easy, 16
mortality, 56, 63–66, 68, 92
My Iron Lung, 16

"Myxamatosis", 18

Nazis, 80–82
neoliberalism, 12, 42
New Testament, 48
niche, 16, 25, 35, 37–40,
        42–43, 92
Nietzsche, Friedrich, 4, 56
Nirvana, 41

O'Brien, Ed, 2, 13, 15
OK Computer, 2, 16, 19, 30,
        45, 59, 69, 90
optimism, 7, 46, 48, 60,
        67–68, 71, 85, 89, 92
"Optimistic", 45, 46
Osborne, Brad, 39, 40

Pablo Honey, 15, 16, 32, 39
pain, 36, 56–57, 59, 61–62,
        68, 86
Parable of the Good
        Samaritan, 67
"Paranoid Android", 4–5,
        45, 86, 88–89
Pärt, Arvo, 57–59, 72
Pitchfork, 11, 20, 22, 31–32
platforms, 41
politics, 5, 33, 93
popularity, 41–42, 57
postmodern, 38
protest, 26, 38, 50–53, 78
Protestant, 76, 79–80
purity, 36–38, 67, 82

Radiohead, 1–34, 35–36,
        39–46, 49–50, 52–
        53, 55, 57, 60–62,
        64- 67, 69, 71–72,
        74, 76, 79–80,
        85–88, 90–94

Rage Against the Machine,
        3
"Reckoner", 2
religion, 4, 7, 27, 37, 43,
        62, 71–73, 77, 84,
        92–93
REM, 16
resistance, 8, 10, 12, 24, 46,
        51–52, 82, 85
resurrection, 56–57, 62, 66,
        68, 92–94
Richter, Gerhard, 57
Rolling Stone, 22

sacred, 38, 47, 50, 57, 72,
        81, 92
Saint Paul, 27, 28
salvation, 11, 54–55, 71, 73,
        84, 89–90, 92
Schneiderman, Davis, 22
science, 16, 54, 63, 65–66
Scripture, 48
secular, 47, 50, 83–84
Selway, Phil, 1, 4, 13, 15, 20
silence, 47, 57, 59, 62, 78
sin, 7, 56, 62, 71, 81
Sistine Chapel, 47
Sittler, Joseph, 55
spirit, 6, 60, 61
Springsteen, Bruce, 5
Stipe, Michael, 57
Stoeger, William, 63
"Street Spirit", 8, 16
suffering, 6, 49, 55–56,
        72, 75
Superbad, 49

technology, 5, 6, 94
The Bends, 10, 16, 35, 39
*The Denial of Death
        (Becker)*, 65

The Eraser, 7, 19
The King of Limbs, 1, 19,
    21, 32
The Little Match Stick Girl,
    72
"The Numbers," 52, 53
theology, 4–8, 10, 12–14,
    25, 34, 37, 46, 53,
    57, 61, 66, 69–71,
    76, 78–79, 82, 91
"There There", 18, 20
Third World, 51
Ticketmaster, 26, 30, 33
"True Love Waits", 18, 20
truth, 4, 6, 12–13, 21, 23,
    25, 28, 35, 40, 48,
    56–57, 62, 64,
    68–69, 80, 90, 92

U2, 3

"Videotape", 4, 94

W.A.S.T.E., 21, 33
weakness, 9, 27, 84, 93
Westhelle, Vitor, 8, 9, 76,
    88, 89
wisdom, 27, 79, 80
Wittkower, D. E., 26
Wolk, Douglas, 22
world, 2, 6, 7, 10, 11, 13,
    18, 27, 29, 31, 36,
    38, 43, 46–48, 54,
    56–57, 59, 62–63,
    65, 71–73, 79–81,
    83–87, 90, 92–94

Yorke, Thom, 1–5, 7–10,
    13–15, 22, 24, 33,
    45, 50–52, 57, 60,
    87, 92